THE UNINVITED

Jeremy Harding is a Senior Editor at the *London Review of Books*. His book, *Small Wars, Small Mercies*, on the last national liberation struggles in Africa, was published by Penguin in 1994.

Embracing globalisation?
— lets put the facts down?

THE UNINVITED

REFUGEES AT THE RICH MAN'S GATE

JEREMY HARDING

P

PROFILE BOOKS
and the
LONDON REVIEW OF BOOKS

First published in book form in Great Britain in 2000 by
Profile Books Ltd
58A Hatton Garden
London EC1N 8LX
www.profilebooks.co.uk

with

London Review of Books
28-30 Little Russell Street
London WC1A 2HN
www.lrb.co.uk

Typeset in Quadraat
Designed by Peter Campbell
Printed and bound in Great Britain by
St Edmundsbury Press, Bury St Edmunds

The moral right of the author has been asserted.

A CIP catalogue record for this book is available
from the British Library.

ISBN 1 86197 211 3

INTRODUCTION

This book began life as a report on the large number of
asylum seekers entering Italy on boats in the late 1990s. It
led to a round-about journey through Europe – Kosovo, Albania, Macedonia, Spain – and then to North Africa. The
result is no longer a report, but the record of a morbid reluctance on the part of the rich world to come to an accommodation with people in distress.

Part I is about refugees trying to reach wealthy countries
now. But to know that the situation in Europe at the start of
the 21st century is nothing new, I have gone back to the period between the two world wars, when refugees were on
the move all over the continent – which led naturally to the
question: does the rise and fall of refugee numbers have any
bearing on the obligations of states to offer sanctuary?

The Cold War was a period of relative calm in Europe.
Now, however, the pressures are more like those of the
1920s and 1930s. In the future, refugee numbers may well
decline. Paradoxically, it is the conservative sensibility, with
its faith in level-headedness and staying the course, that
wants wealthy states to scuttle away from their duty to provide asylum. The wish to bar the door is strong, especially
when the going gets tough, but international obligations
which protect the disadvantaged from panic or indifference
in stable countries may also save the privileged from their
own worst instincts.

I'd thought at first to write only about refugees. But in almost all prosperous states, the asylum debate is sharpened

by the wish to restrict immigration from less developed countries. Part II looks at the predicament of the poorer person who challenges this restriction by entering the rich world illegally – another kind of uninvited visitor who belongs in the broader category of the 'economic migrant'. Illegal 'economic migrants' may have no grounds on which to claim asylum, but the hardships they face in their own countries are as severe as the political persecution from which refugees are fleeing.

Asylum seekers often encounter a new order of hostility in the country of sanctuary. The misfortune of aspiring migrants from underdeveloped parts of the world is much the same: threatened by poverty at home, they find themselves endangered by the indisposition of wealthier societies to let them share in thriving regional and national economies. As I've tried to show, the danger carries well beyond the lives of individuals. Western Europe's project of seclusion has many attractions, but it tends to widen the gulf between the world's rich and the world's poor. It is seriously harmful to both – and it should carry a health warning to that effect.

how to separate the issues?

In the mid-1970s, about 80 million people – roughly 1.5 per cent of the world's population – were living outside the country of their birth. The figure now is closer to 150 million, according to the International Organisation for Migration. It seems implausibly small, but the extent of human movement across borders is hard to monitor – and the figures are a mystery for those of us who have no idea how many people move in and out of our own neighbourhoods in a single day, or a year, or the course of a decade.

Migration is not a simple affair and migrants themselves are as diverse as people who stay put. The banker from Seattle who signs a five-year contract for a post in Berlin is a migrant; so is the lay-out editor in Paris who moves to Moscow to work on a Russian edition of her magazine; so is the labourer from Indonesia or Thailand who is subcontracted to a building site in Brunei; so is the teenage boy from Shanghai indentured to a Chinese crime ring in New York. Refugees, too, are migrants. Often they share their route to safety with others who are not seeking asylum: the smuggling syndicates known as snakeheads, which induct Chinese women into a life of semi-slavery in Europe and the US, also ran dissidents to freedom in the retreat from Tiananmen Square. These things are largely a question of money. Refugees are not necessarily poor, but by the time they have reached safety, the human trafficking organisations on which they depend have eaten up much of their capital. In the course of excruciating journeys, mental and physical resources are also expended – some of them non-renewable.

In the past, the states of Western Europe have shown a generous capacity to take in refugees. The response to forced movement on the Continent itself, from the 1880s to the end of the Second World War, might fairly be seen as impressive. So might the absorption of refugees during the Cold War: far fewer, of course, and mostly from South-East Asia, in keeping with the Cold War commitments of the West. But by the mid-1980s, when numbers started to rise again, states in Western Europe were reviewing their duty to provide asylum. The change was connected with the new availability of one part of the world to another – with the expansion of global access, not least as a result of airline price wars. It occurred at a time when France, Germany, Britain and others had made up their minds that the postwar experiment with immigration from the South was over. Refugees have paid a high price for this decision.

They have also paid for the new prestige of the North American social and economic model – unrivalled now, but all the more conspicuous in its failings. The racially diverse society is a deeply troubling notion in Europe. The grinding together and shifting of peoples – the tectonic population movements that defined the European continent – were already well advanced, and largely settled, by the time the New World became a battleground between the monarchies of Europe and indigenous Americans. For Europeans, the multiracial model of the United States, founded on waves of relatively modern migration, including slave migration – the most lucrative case of human trafficking in history – is flawed. The Right in Europe thinks of it as a triumph of capitalism for which multiculturalism has been a high price to pay. The Left thinks of it as a qualified multicultural success which can never redeem the cost of that triumph.

In both views, the milling of cultures and races and the whirlwind of capitalism are indissociable. Everyone pays grudging homage to the American model of cultural diversity, but European governments of all persuasions are dour about its advantages and alert to its dangers: cities eroded by poverty and profit; the cantonisation of social space; urban and rural societies doubly fractured by ethnicity and class; most forms of negotiation dragged along the runnels of identity politics. And if governments incline to the gloomy view, so do many voters.

Europeans have different ambitions for their social fabric, bound up one way or another with a lingering faith in regulation. Yet those who call for greater control of the global markets and the movement of capital are easily derided, while the wish to restrict free access to wealthier states for people from the South and East is seen as perfectly reasonable. Often the very people who think it a sin to tamper with the self-expression of the markets are the first to call for lower immigration from poorer countries, though in all probability, it would take decades of inward migration to bring about the degree of 'cultural difference' that a bad patch of international trading, a brisk downsizing or a decision by a large corporation to start 'outsourcing' can inject into a social landscape in a year.

It is nothing new for the non-white immigrant, or would-be immigrant, to have to bear the cost of Europe's fears for its own stability, but the EU's wish to keep out asylum seekers is a striking development. Under the International Convention Relating to the Status of Refugees, they are distinguished from other migrants by their ability to demonstrate 'a well-founded fear of being persecuted'. Many who do not qualify for 'Convention status' are protected by other agreements and various forms of temporary

9

asylum, awarded on 'humanitarian grounds'. In practice, however, the distinction between asylum seekers and other kinds of disadvantaged migrant – a distinction designed to shield the refugee from prejudicial factors such as low immigration targets in host states – has been worn away. In Western Europe, refugees have begun to look like beggars at the gate, or even thieves. Since the 1980s, they have lost most lawful means of access to the rich world.

To governments aiming at low levels of immigration from poorer countries, asylum is an exemption that allows too many people past the barriers. Meanwhile, thousands of migrants whose objective is a better standard of living for themselves and those they have left behind are opting for asylum, or plain illegal entry, as a way to outflank restrictive immigration policies. The result is an expensive game of wits being played along the frontiers of the rich world. It is a worldwide contest, in progress anywhere between the state of New Jersey and Taiwan; Queensland and New Mexico. In Europe, the field extends from the Baltic states to the Straits of Gibraltar, from the Aegean to the English Channel. You only have to go to Kent, or the Spanish enclaves in Morocco, or the coast of Puglia in southern Italy to watch the game unfold.

We left the harbour in Otranto just after dark, turned north and ran along the coast towards Brindisi. The boat was crewed by members of Italy's Guardia di Finanza. It was fifty foot or so, with two powerful engines which threshed up the water like a harvester, cutting a straight path visible for half a mile behind us through the rolling waters. The moon, too, threw a line of light, brighter, narrower, scuffed at its edges by the winter swell.

In 1997 and 1998, two or three Guardia reconnaissance

boats were out in the Otranto Channel at any one time, in all but the worst weathers. For most of the night, they combed the waters for boatloads of illegal immigrants from Albania. At the end of the 1990s, the Channel became a game board on which immigrant traffickers and tobacco smugglers pitted their skills against the Guardia, but it was the immigrants – i *clandestini* – who caused the real dismay in Italy. For most of 1998 they were leaving from the Albanian port of Vlorë; then, with Italian police surveillance on the Albanian coast, the departure points were moved. It takes about an hour for a good *scafista* and his partner to get their passengers across roughly 90 km of water. They are crammed aboard *gommoni*, or inflatable rafts, with two outboard motors. The *gommoni* run a gauntlet of detection and danger. The Guardia's boats are equipped with radar; the *scafisti* have to negotiate patches of rough sea at very high speeds; they must also hope for cloud cover. But business is so profitable and, until recently, demand has been so intense, that a clear night has rarely deterred them.

From the deck of a Guardia boat you can see the game board in all its splendour. The wake of the boat and the moonlight traverse the waters like linear markers, setting the terms of the contest. As the *gommoni* scud across the Channel, they must keep clear of these two lines: the giveaway light of the moon and the roaming, telltale wash of the predator. The first two hours of a night patrol are spent in obscure coming and going, the lines of light converging and diverging. As the night draws on and the moon rises, the brighter path begins to fade until there is only a diffuse, milky light covering the water, and the one line, loitering, veering, running straight again, from the back of the boat. It is the record of one crew's efforts to defend Italy's frail territorial integrity, and with it, the integrity of Fortress Europe, bounded by a single external border.

On the Guardia boats, below decks, radar technicians monitor the waters for movement. A regular signal marking every 360 degree scan sounds like the bip of a heartbeat in casualty. In rough weather, the equipment picks up misleading signals. Twice, what might have been a boat turned out to be a piece of flotsam: a large vegetable oil-drum, a reeling assortment of polystyrene packaging. The vessel was well off the Puglia coastline when news came through from the base in Otranto that there were four *gommoni* on the water, within minutes of the Italian beaches.

The lieutenant at the helm took his speed up to about 45 knots, flipping the boat over the waves. Garbled co-ordinates, crumbling with static, came through from the base radio. After a surge of movement that brought us within a kilometre of the coast, we slowed up and hung in the swell. The lieutenant produced a pair of infrared binoculars and gazed through them at the mainland. He handed them across, arranging and rearranging me, until I could pick out the shapes of migrants wading through the shallows, the rubber rafts lying off the beach and the *scafisti* refilling the outboard motors as they prepared for the return journey to Vlorë. It was my first sight of illegal immigrants, tiny, pale and alien, stirring like febrile particles under a microscope. I would have seen them, I suppose, in the way we tend to see them, clambering into our world, importunate, active, invasive, always other than ourselves: *clandestini, i irregolari, extra-comunitari*. Headlights moved from left to right through the trees behind the beach: cars organised by the traffickers to pick up the migrants; maybe a few police vehicles speeding to the scene.

No one in Italy can agree on how many people are in the

country without 'papers'. A recent amnesty for illegals who could prove they'd arrived before March 1998 provoked an uproar when it became clear that fewer than 40,000 irregular migrants would be eligible by the terms of the deal: there were thought to be between five and ten times that number in the country. It is not known how many people entered on the *gommoni* in the late 1990s. Some in the Guardia will tell you that by the middle of 1998, there were up to 40 boats a night; others put it at 25 – which is to say, anything between 500 and 1000 migrants attempting the passage on the coast of Puglia alone. Thousands were coming from Kosovo, Turkish and Iraqi Kurdistan, and places further afield – West Africa, the Horn, the remains of the Soviet Union, Sri Lanka, Pakistan and China. A turmoil of movement has been taking place in the Adriatic, and the Mediterranean as a whole, as thousands of people from the Maghreb make their way up to Sicily or cross the Straits of Gibraltar in fishing boats crammed to the gunwales. It is difficult to know what will stop this movement or how it might be regulated.

In 1998, when Austria held the EU presidency, it suggested in a draft paper on immigration and asylum that the number of migrants to 'the rich, especially Western European, states' exceeds 1.5 million a year. 'The proportion of illegal immigrants in this total,' the paper adds, 'has clearly increased. It must now be assumed that every other migrant in the "first world" is there illegally.' There is no knowing whether this figure is accurate, but one thing is sure: the muddier the conjecture, the better it sticks, and the association with illegality is hard for large numbers of non-nationals or *extra-comunitari* in wealthy EU countries to shed. For asylum seekers this is especially worrying, because so many have had to break the law first in their own country, then in their putative host country, in order to find safety. Often there is no other way.

Paragraph 1, Article 31 of the International Convention Relating to the Status of Refugees recognises that they may be obliged to use illicit means of entry into a safe country – just as they may have to evade customs and immigration checks to get out of their own – and requires that host countries 'shall not impose penalties' on this account. Yet, with the extension of the single European border in the 1990s, asylum seekers who enter a country illegally have come to be seen as a threat to EU, as well as national, security. At the heart of the EU's thinking about refugees lies the imputation of a double criminality: not only do they flout national boundaries, but they consort with criminal trafficking gangs to do so. As signatories to the 1951 Convention, states may not punish asylum seekers for illegal entry, but to associate them persistently with crime is itself an insidious form of penalty. It leads to the presumption that most asylum claims are bogus (if deceit was the means of entry, why should it not be the basis of the whole claim?) and justifies measures designed to deprive them of elementary privileges – some would say, rights.

The huge forced movements of people in Europe during the 20th century were always a cause of anxiety, and often outright hostility, on the part of states that took in refugees. But the record suggests that even very large numbers of refugees can be accommodated without disruption to host countries. During the 1920s and 1930s, France received hundreds of thousands of White Russians and German Jews; in the 1990s, Germany – already deeply committed after reunification – took in more refugees than any other EU member from the former Yugoslavia. The misgivings of wealthy, capitalised states about accommodating refugees are a reaction in the first instance to the manner of their arrival, to the initial cost – housing, school places, social security benefits – and to the tensions that arise, as they have in parts of Germany and Britain, between new groups of refugees and resident communities. The uninvited are a costly nuisance when they first show up: a fact which sharpens official dislike of those who smuggle them in.

The crews of the Guardia di Finanza in Otranto have much to say about the *scafisti*. They will grudgingly admit how much they admire their skill; they will talk morosely about the difficulty of catching them and the leniency with which they are treated by the Italian courts. They think of them chiefly as ruthless profiteers who will put people's lives at risk for gain. Since a clash in 1997 between an Italian coast-guard boat and a large Albanian vessel, when around eighty or ninety migrants were drowned, the Guardia are under instructions to pursue the traffickers only after they have delivered their passengers. The policy is not always observed, but most of the chases in the Channel take place when the *scafisti* are heading for home in empty boats.

A chase is dramatic and largely symbolic – another kind of contest between the cumbersome forces of the state and a more mobile, unencumbered enemy with few allegiances and no terrain to defend. A Guardia boat can manage a top speed of 65 miles an hour. Its quarry is capable of slightly faster bursts, the prow riding up at a rampant angle to the water. Under a handheld searchlight beamed from the Guardia boat, you can see the outboards and the hooded drivers, but as you turn in on the *gommone*, it simply pirouettes in a flurry of spray and slides away. I was on a Guardia boat during one of these chases. The captain forced the *gommone* round several times, turning at full power, until it hit our wake, bouncing wildly over the ridge of ferment, baulking at a great ditch of water on the other side and recovering to steer for home. We made another approach, another turn, a fraction earlier than the last; the *gommone* thrashed across the bows at a tremendous pace and tore into the night; we altered course and picked it up again, pursuing, circling, almost engaging. Things went on in this way until we were halfway to Albania. But it was clear from the first confrontation that the Guardia were up against hopeless odds. In this bruising, violent but strangely abstract hunt, manoeuvrability has a clear advantage.

The organised traffic of people from Albania is abetted in Puglia by the Sacra Corona Unità, one of Italy's four Mafia conglomerates, which also handles tobacco smuggling – now a Guardia priority (as it is for British customs) – and a proportion of the marijuana grown in Albania: the *scafisti* act as couriers. Elsewhere, 'facilitators' offer access to the rich world via lorry, train and sea container. Agents in Asia and Africa receive money for getting people into the high-security areas of airports so that they can stow away in the landing gear of aircraft and die. By the end of the 1990s it was thought that the number of young women being smuggled into the EU every year from the former Eastern bloc and forced into prostitution was in the hundreds of thousands. It is not hard to see why the traffickers are vilified by governments, police and the press. They can foil the defences of the United States and Fortress Europe, carrying a criminal virus into the rich world, a sickness which has its origins – we like to suppose – thousands of miles away.

Some of the best information about traffickers comes from the people who have had to use them. In 1998, at the

Centro Regina Pacis, a summer colony for children con-
verted into short-term accommodation for people caught
on the beaches, I was introduced to a young Kosovar called
Fatmir. He had taught Albanian in a private school in his
village; he was also a Kosovo Liberation Army supporter:
fair game for the Serbians and a likely candidate for asylum
under the terms of the 1951 Convention. In 1998, soon after
his village was bombarded and the school burned down, he
joined an exodus of KLA from the province. They were
heading for Albania. Fatmir took up with a contingent of
about 400 fighters, followed by some 1500 civilians. He
walked for three days across the mountains, but encountered Serbian police at the border. Three of his party were
killed. He now embarked on a ten-day detour, attempting
another route into Albania, but this failed and he made the
five-day journey on foot back across Kosovo and into Mon-
tenegro. There, he and his companions – four brothers and
some cousins – paid 200 Deutschmarks each for a ride in a
kombi down to Lake Shkodër. They paid another 50
Deutschmarks each to be ferried across and, a month or
more later, having arrived in Vlorë, a further 1000 DM or so
for passage on a *gommone*.

The agents who took his money for the last leg of the
journey gave Fatmir the impression that he would be going
straight up to Milan and, from there, through Switzerland
to Germany on forged Italian documents. With him on the
gommone were nine people from Kosovo. Most of the others
were Albanians. The *gommone* was not detected and the passengers, around thirty of them, waded ashore in the dark,
led by an Albanian agent carrying a bag of marijuana. They
followed the agent through the dark into a coppice, hid
until the police had called off a brief helicopter search, and
after a seven-hour walk reached a ruined house in the coun-

tryside. The agent collected more money from all of the passengers and disappeared, instructing them to wait in the house: 'A taxi will come and take you to Milan.' After two hours, a small truck arrived and they wedged themselves inside, but they had only gone a few kilometres when the driver and his mate stopped the vehicle and threw all the Kosovars out. Fatmir and his companions walked to Lecce, thinking they might change some money and take a train north, but they were apprehended at the station and put on a boat back to Albania. Fatmir was returned because he was eager not to claim asylum: a number of people who could petition successfully would rather try to get through Italy undetected and lodge the claim in a neighbouring state, where they have a better network of expatriate contacts who can assist with lodgings, social services and, eventually, jobs. This kind of common sense on the part of asylum seekers is now disparaged by European governments as 'asylum shopping'.

Fatmir's second venture across the Channel some weeks later was a success. Once ashore, he simply went to a police station and announced that he was from Kosovo. He no longer had a Kosovo ID card: it had been removed by an Albanian official on his return from Italy (and sold, he was convinced, to an Albanian who could now pose as a Kosovar in order to claim asylum). He had spoken to dozens of other arrivals and discovered that it was quite common for agents to treat Kosovars – and Kurds – in the way they had treated him, first time around. The agents, he believed, wanted only to maximise their success rate. For Kurds and Kosovars to remain in Italy, it is normally enough for them to make their way to the police, as Fatmir did on his second run, and announce their place of origin, which is why the agents could dump a group from Kosovo by the side of the road, and rob them, without jeopardising their own reputation as effective traffickers or the chances of their clients' remaining in Italy. Albanians, on the other hand, are mostly economic migrants. The EU disapproves of them and, if caught, they are returned as a matter of course by the Italian authorities. For this group, more careful chaperoning by the agents is necessary. The alternative, for an Albanian, is to pose as a Kosovar refugee: Fatmir's Kosovo ID card would have fetched a good deal of money, up in the hundreds of dollars, in Albania.

In Puglia, I became suspicious of the idea that traffickers were a modern embodiment of evil. I didn't doubt their business acumen, or their lack of scruple with lives, but it was reasonable to assume there was another side to the story and in due course I heard it, from a young man called Adem, another resident at Regina Pacis. Adem was from Pristina, the provincial capital of Kosovo. He left in 1998, at the age of 23, after two or three incidents of police harassment. He went overland to Albania and bought a place on a *gommone* for 1750 Deutschmarks – about £600 – but the weather was too much and the boat turned back halfway to Italy. In Vlorë, the passengers waited for another run. Together with a new intake that brought the total to 42, they set off again 12 hours later on a bigger boat. Adem told me in his faltering, Americanised English that the *scafisti* were 'very good guys'. He'd heard about them tipping people overboard at gunpoint and when, on his second run, the Guardia di Finanza approached the boat moments from a beach, he prepared for the worst. Instead, the *scafista* and his mate worked their way about and put off their passengers in the shallows. The Guardia nearly cornered the *gommone* before everyone was off. The *scafisti* flipped it around at full throttle and lit away from the beach, with a man and two young children still on board. Again, Adem expected to see them dump their charges in the high waters a hundred metres from the beach, but they took the *gommone* into another patch of shallows and helped them over the side. The Guardia boat was in hot pursuit and Adem believed the *scafisti* were taking 'a big risk' when they set the last three passengers down.

There are nonetheless few Schindlers among the modern traffickers in human beings, and the money is good: one *gommone* with 30 passengers safely delivered represents about £20,000 in fees; it has been suggested that the business of illegal migrant trafficking, worldwide, is worth between $5 and $7 billion a year – and a significant part of the business involves a second tier of profiteering, in the West, as young women from outside the EU are herded into the sex industry: refugees have always kept strange company. We think of agents, traffickers and facilitators as the worst abusers of asylum seekers. But when they set out to extort from their clients, when they cheat them or dispatch them to their deaths, they are only enacting an entrepreneurial version of the disdain which asylum seekers suffer at the hands of far more powerful enemies – those who terrorise them and those who are determined to keep them at arm's length. Human traffickers are simply vectors of the contempt which exists at the two poles of the asylum seeker's journey; they take their cue from the attitudes of warlords and dictators, on the one hand, and, on the other, of wealthy states whose citizens have come to see generosity as a vice. When traffickers treat their clients properly, however, they interrupt the current of contempt. Above all, they save lives. In the end, the question of good or bad intentions is less important than the fact that the *scafisti* and others like them provide a service for desperate people, to whom most other avenues have been closed.

This is the meaning of the terse exchange that millions of us have watched at least once in the movie *Casablanca*, shortly before the love interest sweeps in, arm-in-arm with the suave paragon of anti-Nazi struggle. It is 1942; Casablanca is full of refugees who have taken passage from Marseilles to Oran and come overland in the hope of obtaining a visa to Lisbon. Ugarte (Peter Lorre), a forger and procurer of documents, asks Rick to look after two sets of safe-conduct papers until his clients arrive. 'You despise me, don't you?' he says to Rick. 'You object to the kind of business I do, huh? But think of all those poor refugees who must rot in this place if I didn't help them. But that's not so bad. Through ways of my own, I provide them with exit visas.'

'For a price, Ugarte,' Rick replies. 'For a price.'

In human trafficking, the price is the main consideration, but it is not everything. Traffickers enjoy playing cat and mouse with immigration authorities. In the mid-1990s, the exiled Somali novelist Nuruddin Farah began to investigate the state of his fellow nationals after the fall of Siyad Barre. Many were refugees in Kenya. Others had made it to Europe, North America and the Gulf. Farah spoke to several of the traffickers who had helped them and soon discovered the relish with which the 'battle of wits' was joined. In Italy, he met a '*xambaar* carrier' or trafficker, once a professor of biochemistry, who was now officially a 'resident' in one European country and a 'refugee' in another. 'What matters,' he told Farah, 'is that the doors are closed . . . and we, as carriers, are determined to open them.' Another *xambaar* carrier in Milan told him that trafficking was a kind of 'dare' – a challenge taken up in the dismal refugee camps in East Africa, where many Somali carriers have had to subsist in the first stages of exile. Carrying, he said, was largely a way of helping people to snub the rich nations, 'who frustrate their desire to leave a hell-hole of a country like Kenya by placing obstacles in their path all the way from the starting point of their journey down to the cubby-holes which they call home here in Milan'.

The game of wits, the challenge, the whole rigmarole of clandestine entry – these have never been far from the refugee's experience, but it is only since the 1980s, when Europe embarked with new zeal on its project of seclusion, that they have become so all-encompassing. Among the most important changes is the fact that rich countries now require a visa from citizens wishing to travel from places which are likely to generate asylum seekers. Britain, for example, imposed visa requirements for people travelling from Sri Lanka in 1985 (and broke with a cherished Commonweath tradition in doing so), from Algeria in 1990, from Sierra Leone in 1994 and from Colombia in 1997. It is, of course, very dangerous for someone who is being targeted by a regime, or an insurrectionary group, or a religious movement, to be seen presenting themselves at a foreign embassy day after day in the hope of obtaining a visa. Even if the embassy is not under surveillance, there are likely to be local staff who will report the application. Safer, for those who can afford airline tickets, to think of a destination that does not require an entry visa, buy a ticket that involves a stopover in the country in which they wish to claim asylum, and make the claim in transit. But this option is being closed off by means of the Direct Airline Transit Visa,

22

So what is the soln

introduced by Britain in 1998 when a group of Kosovars claimed asylum while they were in transit through London. Travellers from over a dozen countries are now required to have these visas if their flights stop over in Britain, and in 1999 the Finnish presidency of the EU proposed to extend this policy to other states by means of a standard-format transit visa.

In addition, airlines must pay high fines for carrying anyone whose papers are not in order, as well as the cost of returning them to their point of departure. 'Carriers' liability', as it is known, is an American idea, which can be found in a Bill that went before the Senate immigration committee in 1903 and called for deportations of undesirable immigrants 'at the expense of the steamship or railroad company which brought them'. When carriers' liability reappeared in the 1980s, the US again took the lead, but there were now a number of wealthy countries willing to follow suit. Airline companies had once been a neutral – which is to say, benevolent – force from the asylum seeker's point of view; ground staff might even intervene discreetly in cases where local security in some torrid dictatorship tried to prevent a dissident boarding a plane. This has changed. The risk of incurring high penalties has forced carriers to act as a screening agency on behalf of governments. By January 2000 the British Government had widened the scope of liability: it now applies to the Eurostar rail link and to haulage companies whose vehicles are found to contain stowaways.

None of this would be so serious if the UN's resettlement programmes could bring refugees to safety. But their application is narrow. Strictly speaking, to be eligible for resettlement, a person must already be in a country 'of first asylum' and still be at risk – like many Somalis in Kenya –

or unable to integrate in the longer term. This rules out hundreds of thousands of people, not yet recognised as refugees according to the terms of the 1951 Convention. The resettlement programme is also modest. In the late 1970s, the UN High Commissioner for Refugees was resettling nearly a quarter of a million people a year (most of them from Indochina), or roughly one in four of the world's refugees. By the end of the 1990s, resettlement involved fewer than 30,000 people – around one in every 500.

Little by little, the routes which asylum seekers once took to safety have been choked off. The formidable growth in underground 'travel agencies' – document forgers, chaperones, drivers, boatmen – is the consequence. They are the material result of Europe's dreary pastoral fantasy, in which the EU resembles an Alpine valley, surrounded by impregnable, snow-capped mountains. For most asylum seekers who wish to reach Europe, being smuggled to sanctuary has become the only option.

At the harbour in Otranto there are two short rows of pre-fabricated huts and containers for illegals who have been caught, most of them on the beach, a handful inland. They arrive at the huts drenched and chilled to the marrow. They are shivering, terrified, nearly ecstatic – a state induced by the journey and the fact of having survived it. Their eyes are bright, feverish, inquiring, their faces transfigured by a combination of exhaustion, curiosity and surprise. It's as though they'd tumbled slowly and painfully to earth through rain-logged skies and couldn't quite grasp that they'd survived the impact of landing. Jeans, shirts, pullovers are set out to dry between the huts and, after an hour or so, the men begin milling about, while the women sit with their heads bowed and the children sleep.

It is 5 a.m. There are dozens of detainees in the huts. Two Albanians who are sure to be sent back take out their documents: they have wives in Italy and children attending Italian schools; they have work contracts and Italian tax returns, the sodden evidence of their right to reside in Italy. One is a building labourer, the other a mechanic. When the labourer heard that his mother had taken sick in Tirana, his friend accompanied him back. The time came to return to Italy, but they couldn't get the authorisation from the Italian Embassy and anyhow, they explained, it is hard to take the legal route to Italy on the ferry that plies the Channel daily. The *scafisti* soften the ticketing companies and harbour authorities with a mixture of threats and incentives, to ensure that very few passengers avail themselves of the ferry and demand for the *gommoni* remains high. But these two men, who are legally entitled to stay in Italy, attempted illegal entry and that is sufficient reason to send them back. (Imagine a diligent servant lodging in the house of the family he works for. He has to leave for a day, on business, but loses his key. He arrives late at night and enters by a window at the back. The family dismisses him.) The strain on their faces is no longer the strain of fatigue. It has cost them over the odds to get to Otranto and now all their outlay is squandered. They point again and again to their documents, place them in my hands, chivvy me into longer, more fastidious inspection, and when I hand them back, they, too, stare at them, as though they were turning to pulp.

By 7 a.m. medics, finger-printers and interpreters are arriving at Otranto harbour. People are examined for injuries. Migrants often sustain fractures wading ashore in the dark. Children can be concussed, or more seriously damaged, by the repetitive jolting of the boats at high speed on rough seas. In one of the huts, plywood table tops have been set across oil-drums and forensic staff are preparing to take fingerprints. The migrants shuffle down the line with their hands extended. The abrupt introduction of the illegal alien to the grudging host state begins. In this parody of greeting, gloved hands reach out to bare hands, seize them, flatten them down on an ink block, lift them across the table-top and flatten them again onto a square of paper. Four sets of prints are taken from each person, then a photograph. A group of Kurdish men, some in stone-washed denims, others in crumpled check turn-ups from their overnight bags, dig their knuckles into a tub of industrial cleansing jelly and climb out of the hut, wringing their blackened hands. A truck arrives with sacks of sandwiches and cases of mineral water. Briefly the sight of food rouses the detainees; dejection and reticence give way to energy and assertion. Men come forward to skirmish on behalf of wives, sisters, children. As disorder threatens, a detachment of *carabinieri* cajoles them into silence.

There are 60 detainees in all. About a third are Albanians, who will be sent back on the ferry. The rest are Kosovars and Kurds, who will be shepherded onto buses and driven up the coast to the Centro Regina Pacis, to be quartered and processed, and eventually released into Italy with a short-stay permit or leave to remain while Rome considers their asylum applications. The figures for last night's game in the Otranto Channel are now through: 12 landings and 201 detentions along the coast of Puglia. But many will have got away. It is a Sunday morning. Rain drives down on the prefab huts. Grey seas fret at the harbour walls. As the first contingent of shivering Kurds prepares to board a waiting bus, a dull church bell starts tolling for Mass.

Whether they'll live or die must, at some point on the journey, become a more pressing question for illegal entrants into EU countries than whether they will find a foothold in the rich world. These journeys are dangerous. But to be driven by attrition is to prefer the devil you don't know, or to give him the benefit of the doubt, and for those who buy passage on the *gommoni*, the devil is vaguely familiar in any case. Rumour and precedent keep the *scafisti* in business. This form of passage is relatively low risk. The bigger boats which fill up with passengers along the shores of the eastern Mediterranean and drift around with hundreds of people on board waiting for the moment to abandon them on the Italian coast are another matter. Death from thirst, sickness, hunger or a full-scale disaster are pressing possibilities.

About three hours after the buses loaded with Kurds and Kosovars left for Regina Pacis on that bitter Sunday morning, a 200-tonne vessel under an Albanian flag dropped anchor south of Otranto, off Santa Maria de Leuca. The captain and most of the crew got away in an inflatable raft, consigning their passengers to Italian jurisdiction, and the Guardia di Finanza began shuttling them off the boat in lighters and reconnaissance craft. The captain had been cruising the coasts of Greece and Albania for two weeks, but some of the passengers had probably been at sea for longer, languishing in an even larger boat anchored off the coast of Turkey, before being decanted into this elderly cargo ship.

Hundreds of bystanders waited on the quays in the lashing rain, watching the migrants disembark. There were many exhausted women and children coming off the boat. One Guardia shuttle consisted entirely of Africans. On the gangways, a ravaged young man lifted his face and bared his parched mouth to the downpour. To a barrage of questions he replied that he was from Sierra Leone and that he'd been travelling for three months. He flicked one hand gracefully, dismissively, at about the level of his forehead: 'Up, up.'

He meant that he and his friends had come overland from West Africa. I asked where they'd boarded ship, but the police shut the conversation down. That night I drove along the coast through a violent storm to Regina Pacis, to find out more, but the gates were barred by *carabinieri*. After half an hour an official appeared and read out a provisional tally of arrivals: 169 from Turkey, probably Kurds, four from Iraq, three Afghans, 17 from Sierra Leone, 29 from Guinea-Bissau, one from the Democratic Republic of Congo and another from Senegal.

In the course of 24 hours in deep winter, with Italian security already beginning to deploy in Albania and the Italian Government more resolute than it had been throughout the hectic summer of 1998, 400 illegal migrants had entered the country. The figure does not include those who made their way off the beaches of Puglia without being detected. Statistics for the following year showed no let-up: by October 1999, over 20,000 illegal migrants had been apprehended and for every one of those, the Guardia di Finanza estimated, two or three would have slipped through the net.

This is not the first time that Europe has become a place of passage and confusion. In 1937, with one massive displacement of people following another in the heart of the continent and points east, the Royal Institute of International Affairs in London commissioned a comprehensive survey of refugee movements. To superintend the project, it appointed John Hope Simpson, a persuasive and highly energetic man who had worked in India and Palestine, directed the National Flood Relief programme in China and served as vice-president of the Refugee Settlement Commission in Athens. In the summer of 1938, Simpson published a preliminary report of his team's findings. By the time a full text was ready for the presses in October, he was forced to note in his preface that the annexation of Austria had now 'strained the capacity of absorption of neighbouring countries to breaking point', while the annexation of Sudeten areas of Czechoslovakia had created 'yet another most serious problem, the full effects of which are not yet measurable'. A report commissioned at a moment which the Institute might justifiably have thought to be the highpoint of the 'refugee problem' was superseded on the eve of publication by a further flurry of stateless people and evacuees clamouring for sanctuary. Yet the findings of Simpson and his colleagues on refugee movements in the preceding years and on reception and settlement in host countries, were so carefully researched and presented that the finished document, which runs to 600 pages, remains a model of what has come to be known as 'refugee studies'. It also has a bearing on the great refugee movements we are witnessing now.

Simpson's mainstay in France was H.W.H. Sams, a gifted investigator decorously referred to in the report as 'Mr Sams'. France, Simpson noted, was 'par excellence the country of refuge in Western Europe' and Sams had his work cut out to account for the hundreds of thousands of refugees from Russia, Germany, Armenia, Saarland, Republican Spain and, as time went on, from Fascist Italy. For most of the 1920s, a high demand for labour worked in favour of refugee 'integration'. Depression did away with that propitious circumstance – it also marked a reversal in

France's vigorous pro-immigration policy. By the mid-1930s, however, labour was once again an issue: indeed, with the population little more than half that of its huge, industrialised and militarised neighbour to the east, something of a national security imperative. On the other hand, tailoring the location of refugees to the precise contours of demand, before and after the Depression, was impossible and would, in any case, have been a delicate matter, even though popular animosity towards them and outright ill-treatment were common enough. Of the large numbers of Russians entering France after the Bolshevik Revolution, a proportion were thoroughly marginalised. Sams reported that in Marseilles, those who worked on the docks 'are amongst the dregs of the cosmopolitan population' of the city. In Lyons, which had one of the biggest Russian colonies, 45 per cent of the refugees were unemployed and living in 'great poverty'. Every night, along the banks of the Rhone, about 100 'bridge-dwellers' were sleeping rough.

Conditions of work, even for the many refugees who had it, were often dismal. Lyons, with its high numbers of émigré unemployed, may have been one of Sams's 'black spots' for sickness, but so was Billancourt, where there had once been 8000 Russians in the Renault works. Sams gave heart strain and TB as the main causes of illness in the refugee workforce. Problems of labour rivalry also arose. The two conventions of 1933 and 1938 to which France was a signatory urged that 'restrictive laws' governing foreign labour 'shall not be applied in all their severity to refugees'. The French, however, entered a reservation in the margin about foreign labour quotas – the same quotas, Mr Sams noted drily, which meant that only 15 per cent of the musicians in a well known balalaika orchestra could be Russian. The quota system was left in place by the Front Populaire, making it hard for new refugees with qualifications to find a position, while political attitudes tended to harden in industry. Sams hints that the refugees in Lyons suffered at the hands of the French Communist Party. 'The Russians,' he reported, were regarded as 'enemies of Soviet Russia' (a very different objection from the one raised by Lyonnaise prostitutes sixty years later when the first young women with Kosovo ID papers began appearing on the quays).

Still, there was work and, under the Front Populaire, a growing culture of social provision. 'In general,' Sams reported from Moselle, 'any Russian with the willingness to work and good health can earn a living.' Former German nationals, too, found sanctuary in France, which in the third quarter of 1933, received between 30,000 and 60,000 refugees from Nazism. Many remained for several years, others moved on to Palestine, Latin America, the US and South Africa. The figures began to fall in 1937, but by now 6 per cent of the population were of foreign origin and there were still refugees coming in from Germany, Austria and Spain, including 'wounded or incapacitated German members of the International Brigades'.

It was the crisis in the Austro-Hungarian, Russian and Ottoman Empires, and the fretwork of successor states created after their demise, that gave Simpson and his team such a wealth of human material to consider. Already, between the 1880s and the eve of the Great War, enormous numbers of Jews had been driven west by the ferocity of the pogroms. By the time the Ottoman Empire had been divested, the survivors of the Armenian genocide of 1915–16 were scattered in camps from Sofia to Damascus. In the 1920s, thousands of Kurds followed the Armenians out of Turkey to settle in Syria, the Lebanon and Iraq. By one count, a million and a half Russians were displaced by the Bolshevik Revolution; a third of these were still stateless by World War Two. With the dismantling of Austria-Hungary and the formation of the Baltic states, more Europeans swelled the ranks of *apatrides*, or stateless persons; others found that they were now members of precarious minorities with marginal rights in new political entities, confected by the postwar treaties.

At the end of World War Two, with the retrenchment of the Western empires, mass movement was largely assigned out of Europe: to India, Palestine, Indochina — and thereafter to zones of contention where the superpowers had leaseholder status and a steely readiness to wage war by proxy. During the Cold War, three million people left their homes in Cambodia, Laos and Vietnam, five million left Afghanistan, a million or more were uprooted in Central America, two to three million Palestinians dug deeper into exile; in Africa, where there are still nearly seven million refugees and many more people displaced inside their own borders, a long moment of upheaval began.

The end of hostilities between the Soviet Union and the West brought hundreds of aid workers and dozens of refugee monitors – the successors of John Hope Simpson and Mr Sams – back from the tropics to Europe. The dramatic character of events in 1989 and the years that followed gave them a singular cast, but in the Baltic countries and elsewhere it was a smeared mirror-image of interwar statelessness that now reappeared, as a series of successor states came into being after the collapse of Communism. Punitive rules of citizenship denied 700,000 Russian-speakers national status in Latvia and 500,000 in Estonia. By the end of 1996, the UNHCR was alarmed by the 'significant numbers' of Slovaks and Roma rendered stateless, in effect, by the creation of Slovakia and the Czech Republic.

In the 1930s, Yugoslavia and Czechoslovakia had been exemplary hosts to large refugee populations. It was now the turn of former Yugoslav and Czechoslovak nationals – Yugoslavs, above all – to spill across new boundaries in search of refuge. Many of the elements that had led to the massive evictions of the interwar years were once again in place, but the idea of sanctuary had withered: Europe had forgotten the codes of conduct in moments of crisis. And in trying to reckon with the wars in Yugoslavia, it was unsure whether the Balkans were really a part of the new amnesiac Europe at all: might they not simply be Slav lands caught in an eternal dichotomy of fracture and Oriental despotism – and foundering in the useless politics of memory?

Western Europe's heightened sense of the other – both fearful and condescending – shaped its reluctance to intervene in any decisive way in Bosnia, but at the end of the 1990s, with very high numbers of refugees already exiled from the former Yugoslavia and thousands more now arriving from Kosovo, it was impossible to quarantine the Balkans any longer. The many asylum seekers who breached the fortress, and to whom, in the end, Germany and others opened their doors, were a pressing consideration in the Nato air campaign. A regime that had confined the effects of its misdeeds within its own borders might have fared better, but Slobodan Milosevic's policies were foisting large numbers of terrified people on prosperous nations that wanted nothing to do with them. That was one of the issues that the European members of Nato had in mind when they spoke of a 'humanitarian crisis'. Tens of thousands of Kosovars had already lodged asylum claims in the EU before Nato began its air strikes. The Albanian *scafisti* ferried hundreds across the Otranto Channel every week, while others struck out overland for Western Europe. The EU looked on with growing dismay.

Yet the extraordinary deportations with which Serbia responded to the Nato intervention made these movements look trifling by comparison. In a matter of months, the number of deportees in Macedonia and Albania stood at around half a million. This was by no means the biggest post-World War Two eviction in Europe – the 'return' of Germans from Poland and Sudetenland involved far higher numbers – yet it was probably the most shocking. The speed and intensity of the Kosovo deportations gave them the appearance of rapid flight from a natural disaster. By spelling out the morbid continuity between the earlier part of the century and its close, the exodus also seemed to suggest that the 'great events' of history which occurred first as tragedy were in no way destined to repeat themselves as farce.

There were fewer media organisations on hand, of course, to record the earlier movements of people on a similar scale in Europe. To get from Skopje, the Macedonian capital, to the country's border with Kosovo during Nato's bombing campaign, you had to negotiate a double barrier of police and military roadblocks and then, as you approached the gantries of Macedonian customs and immigration, a vast array of foreign journalists. The field at Blace, where perhaps forty thousand refugees were confined by the Macedonian Government, became the focus of round-the-clock scrutiny by hundreds of digital camcorders and telephoto lenses. It was as though the world had dispatched emissaries to record the arrival of an unknown life form, now evolving in a vast crater of mud and bodily waste. The refugees were cordoned off, victims of a threefold dispossession: forced from their homes and relieved of their belongings by Milosevic; denounced and immobilised by the Government of Macedonia; inspected – though hardly addressed – by the media. Stateless, defenceless and finally voiceless. Eventually, posing as emergency workers to slip through the police lines, the press were able to enter the field and talk directly with people who had no idea what was about to happen to them.

Gaps began appearing in the screen of objectification thrown up around them, but these did nothing to alleviate the mixture of apprehension and dislike with which they were greeted in Macedonia. Here, above all, they were seen as a potential threat to national stability (and 'Slav' ascendancy), already under pressure from the country's Albanian minority. The desultory tones of Western governments – slow to offer support to the Macedonians in the face of this extraordinary crisis – gave rise to anger. There was much to extenuate the reaction of this little country to the overwhelming influx of refugees – it was no worse than the worst reactions in wealthier countries to the arrival of Kosovars – but in the end, it looked very much like a version of the same hostility that had driven them from their homes in the first place.

In *The Origins of Totalitarianism*, Hannah Arendt remarked that 'those whom the persecutor had singled out as the scum of the earth – Jews, Trotskyites etc – actually were received as scum of the earth everywhere.' She was writing about the 'denationalisations' of the 1930s under Hitler and Stalin. The Kosovan refugees fleeing into Albania were spared the cruelty they encountered in Macedonia. They came in carts, towed by tractors, along the flaring snowline of Pastrik, down into a country that existed only in name, but which was once the lodestone of every militant Kosovar's irredentist dreams. Here they were lodged by distant Albanian cousins: in Kukes, in the north of Albania, I saw 26 people living in an apartment that a family of four could have managed in Slough or Sarcelles. Yet there was a bitter aftertaste to this draft of hospitality, for it proved that blood and filiation are the best guarantees of sanctuary and that outside their clan, refugees have little to fall back on. In millions of cases, to be an asylum seeker is to be a stranger on trial. He is accused of nothing more palpable than his intentions, but these are assumed to be bad and the burden of proof rests with the defence. The ethnic Albanians forced out of Kosovo into Macedonia were not even put in the dock.

Reviewing what had happened during the 1930s, Arendt wrote at length about the capacity of nation-states to project their prejudices. (Of these she had first-hand knowledge: she had left Germany in 1933, after a run-in with the Gestapo, and worked in Paris for a youth organisation, arranging the transfer of Jewish orphans to Palestine.) She believed that it was a simple matter for a totalitarian regime to ensure that the people it had turned into outcasts were received as outcasts wherever they went. She refers to an extract from a circular put out in 1938 by the German Ministry of Foreign Affairs to its diplomatic staff abroad: 'The influx of Jews in all parts of the world invokes the opposition of the native population and thereby forms the best propaganda for the German Jewish policy . . . The poorer and therefore more burdensome the immigrating Jew is to the country absorbing him, the stronger the reaction of the country.' Arendt was confident that this is more or less what happened. 'Those whom persecution had called undesirable,' she wrote, 'became the *indésirables* of Europe.'

Sweeping, certainly, but her remarks catch the drift of

the refugee's central misfortune: that he is shuttled along a continuum of abuse, a victim of 'persecuting governments' who can 'impose their values' on other governments – even those who oppose them in fact or on principle. For Kosovars who fled to Albania, clan and language broke the continuum. But most of the refugees and displaced people produced by the break-up of Yugoslavia, including the Serbs, have run the gamut of opprobrium that begins when a regime decides that a proportion of its people are guilty of 'subversions of brotherhood and unity' or are simply 'barbarian' and continues when those people are denounced by a local newspaper in a country of asylum a thousand miles away as 'human sewage', which is how the *Dover Express* described the Kosovan and Kurdish refugees holed up on the south coast of England in 1998. The government of a country of asylum may not share the views of its doughty fourth estate, but it is bound to take them into account as it draws up measures, such as those introduced in Britain, to keep asylum seekers at bay.

Depriving refugees of their assets before they flee, in order to ensure a hostile reception in countries that receive them is harder now than it was between the wars. Army and police can raze their houses, kill their livestock, strip them of their jewelry, steal their cars and cash and destroy their papers – all of this and worse occurred in Kosovo – but they cannot intervene so easily in the network of contacts that persecuted communities build up abroad. Once a pattern of departure is set down, as it has been in Turkish and Iraqi Kurdistan, Sri Lanka, Bosnia and Kosovo, the refugee can follow the thread of survival through the labyrinth with help from friends and relatives outside the country who are ready to put up money for the journey or provide support in the early stages of adaptation.

That pattern of support is as old as migration itself. What is new is the ease with which many persecuted people can move money out of a country before they leave. Once a community under pressure grasps the enormity of its situation, as ethnic Albanians in Kosovo did at the end of the 1980s, it begins to evacuate resources. The crucial transfer is psychological. When hope – the simple idea that circumstances might improve – is no longer possible in situ, it becomes fugitive. As it migrates across borders, the able-bodied and the educated go with it: often the middle classes are the most visible dissidents and among the first to leave. Redoubts are established in the wider world; jobs are forthcoming and, in time, others consider leaving. The rhythms are those of straightforward economic migration, with a smaller flow of remittances to the homeland: it is pointless to remit earnings to a place where they can be pillaged. On the contrary, the more who leave, the greater the transfers out, as those who remain convert their wealth into hard currency and place it abroad with the help of others who have left. In due course, the free expression of political views, outlawed at home, becomes possible outside: journals, meetings, fund-raisers, levies, numbered accounts into which donations to the cause can be paid. This was the case of the Eritrean and Palestinian exiles during the 1970s and 1980s and the Kosovar community in Switzerland during the 1990s. It is also one of the reasons people can raise the fees charged by traffickers.

The poor refugee is just as disadvantaged as the poor person in a stable social arrangement. In Yugoslavia, greater numbers of Serbs have been hounded from pillar to post than any other ethnic or 'national' group. Indeed, by the end of the 1990s there was no larger group of displaced Europeans. Yet of the 600,000 Serbs who have been uprooted once and, in some cases, several times, only a small proportion have known how to salvage their wealth. They have, too, been prey to the regime in Belgrade. If Milosevic wanted to strip Kosovo Albanians of their citizenship – for which few of them had much enthusiasm anyhow – he also used the misfortunes of other Yugoslavs, exiled by the wars in Bosnia and Croatia, to slow down the unravelling of Yugoslavia. Their hardship was as severe as anything faced by the many Yugoslavs who made their way towards the rich world.

The Marinkovic family were interlopers in Kosovo. They arrived in Pristina in 1995. Their new home lay under the shadow of a pale ochre high rise: the military police headquarters, a source of comfort to Kosovo's Serbian minority and an object of loathing to Albanians. Marinkovic and his relatives lived together in a large room with five beds in a wooden hut full of other Serbs, like them, from the Krajina. There were several such barracks, disposed around the police building in an overground warren. They had once contained more than a hundred people but, by 1998, when I met the Marinkovic family, there were no more than forty. Old Djuro Marinkovic, his daughter Anka and their dependants were refugees from the remains of their own country, until Croatia's independence was recognised in 1992. Three years later, when Croatian forces retook the Krajina, they were thrust into exile with thousands of others. A refugee is, by definition, someone who has fled beyond the borders of his own country – someone who knows that the only option is to head for open water. For the Marinkovic family, the process was different. Yugoslavia simply drained around them. Federal boundaries suddenly became sand spits denoting the frontiers of new sovereign entities. The 200,000 Kosovo Albanians who abandoned their villages during the Serbian repression of 1998 were mostly 'internally displaced', hiding within their own province – circumscribed by the national frontier of Serbia and the federal frontier of the addled Yugoslavia. But when Djuro Marinkovic and his fellow Serbs from the Krajina fled towards Belgrade in 1995, they were making for the capital of a state whose jurisdiction no longer obtained in their place of origin. In the cold eye of history, they were like any Europeans undone by the vicissitudes of the 1920s and 1930s.

Marinkovic was 62 when he was uprooted from the Krajina. He'd had a farmstead of about 15 acres. He kept sheep, pigs and cattle and tended an orchard. When the crisis came, he got his family away without mishap. On their arrival in Belgrade, they registered as refugees and were eventually transferred to Pristina. Other options had been mooted, but in Belgrade they were promised that if they moved to Kosovo, they would be housed by the Republic of Serbia. That seemed to clinch it. Marinkovic, his wife, their daughter and her two children became the willing victims of Milosevic's forlorn attempt to shift the ethnic balance in Kosovo in favour of the Serbian minority. By the mid-1990s, several thousand Krajina Serbs had been dumped in the province like so much ethnic ballast.

Marinkovic's life had been a long, fumbling, painful descent into the basement of Europe and, after three years in Kosovo, he was ready to admit that he was in the dark – that everything had gone wrong. He told me that he had been interned in a Croatian camp for Serbs in 1941; that in the same year his father had been murdered by Ustashe guards; that his older brother, a Partisan, had been killed in the course of duty and that his mother had become a drunkard.

As a boy of nine or ten, he said, he had worked with the Partisans, setting fires in the fields to guide in Allied planes. This, in turn, put him in mind of how the enemy had laid false fires to mislead the pilots – and the memory of these fires brought him round to the subject of Milosevic, the deceiver; the man that he, Marinkovic, should never have taken at his word. In Kosovo there was nothing. The old man lived in miserable conditions, surrounded by angry ethnic Albanians; he received a pittance as a guardian on a building site; his family depended on a regular international aid package of basic foodstuffs.

In the summer of 1999, after the Serbian withdrawal from Kosovo, I looked for Marinkovic in Pristina. Before the bombings, there were two places, apart from the cramped barracks, where you could find Krajina Serbs. One was a miserable hotel, permanently under guard, the other a stone building up towards the city's mosques. Since Nato's entry under the guise of KFOR, the hotel had changed hands and the stone building had been boarded up. Where the Marinkovic family had lived, the sun beat down on the charred remains of the huts. A large radio mast in the police complex had been targeted during the sorties. It lay lengthways in front of the ruins.

The Marinkovic family had not been long in Kosovo – a little less than four years. Now, in all likelihood, they had been pushed back into Serbia proper, along with hundreds of families driven out under the new dispensation, and scores of the Roma. As the Serbs headed north, hundreds of Gypsies – also targets of ethnic Albanian fury — began heading west, replacing Kosovars on the boats from Albania or making their way by other routes towards France and Britain, to join the tide of 'human sewage' in which Dover, a town of some 35,000 inhabitants hosting around a thousand refugees at the time, imagined it was foundering.

Kosovo was a storm in the microclimate of crisis and asylum in Europe. As it cleared, the issues that were pressing during the Gulf War and the conflict in Bosnia became visible again. The names of places like Blace in Macedonia and Kukes in Albania have already been replaced by others; there will be successors to figures like Milosevic and Saddam; a UNHCR emergency in the former Yugoslavia is followed by another on the borders of East Timor, then Chechnya; each emergency gives way to a new one, which we might or might not have foreseen. The numbers of Kosovars on the *gommoni* from Albania have already diminished, but others have replaced them: Kurds, Iraqis, Sri Lankans, the kinds of people who waded ashore on the beaches of Italy at the end of the 1990s, mixed inextricably with Roma from Kosovo and economic migrants from Albania proper. Governments in 'receiving countries' have to hold to the belief that at some time or other the forced movement of people can be reduced, especially in a world where a culture of human rights enforcement and 'good governance' has begun to nag at old bulwarks of impunity such as national sovereignty. But there is nothing to suggest that they will. In the meantime, the same sovereign status that has been challenged by military means in the former Yugoslavia can be challenged by law in the wealthy democracies, above all in the EU, where recourse to the European Court of Human Rights may produce outcomes that go against an individual state's preference for minimal intakes of refugees.

The central international instrument designed to protect refugees is the Convention of 1951 (it was extended beyond its original geographical limitation to Europe by a Protocol in 1967). The definition of a refugee is to be found in Chapter 1, Article 1, which states that the Convention shall apply to anyone outside 'the country of his nationality' as a result of a 'well-founded fear of being persecuted for reasons of race, religion, nationality, membership of a particular social group or political opinion and is unable or, owing to such fear, unwilling to avail himself of the protection of that country'. The question is how a contracting party goes about the business of interpretation. The wording of Chapter 1, Article 1 might be taken to mean that only persecution by a state makes an applicant eligible for 'Convention status'. This would rule out persecution by a warlord or a rebel insurgency and so, for example, hundreds of thousands of Angolans who lived in terror of Jonas Savimbi's Unita movement would not qualify for Convention status, though followers of Unita – largely drawn from one 'ethnicity' (indeed, one 'social group') – who were threatened with retribution by the Angolan Army or round-ups by the police, might well. Again, an Algerian journalist who feared for her life at the hands of the Groupe Islamique Armé would be less likely to qualify than someone who was known to have voted 'Islamic' in the early 1990s and was at risk of summary justice from state paramilitaries.

These are extreme examples, but the notion that state persecution alone defines a Convention refugee predominated in France and Germany during the last part of the 20th century. Other countries, such as Canada, the UK and Ireland, have taken the broader view that Convention status should apply to people that a state is unable to protect – which would mean not only that the potential victim of a Unita atrocity and the Algerian journalist were eligible, but that a victim of sexual harassment or domestic violence might become a Convention refugee. (Canada has given Convention status to Chinese families as a result of the 'one child only' policy in China.) And it could well be, according to a signatory's interpretation, that the term 'social group' covered broad minorities such as gays, or women under attack by a particular regime – the Taliban, for instance. In Britain, the Home Office has now been forced by the courts to consider women fleeing persecution under customary marriage laws as plausible asylum seekers.

Interpretations of the Convention reflect the political priorities of signatory states. Above all, they give an indication of how a state views immigration in general. A country such as Canada, with a more obvious use for migration than a country like Britain, is likely to take a more generous view of asylum. The real effects of this difference are remarkable. In 1996, Canada deemed that 76 per cent of applicants from the former Zaire, 81 per cent from Somalia and 82 per cent from Sri Lanka qualified for Convention status. In the same year in Britain, only 1 per cent of applicants from Zaire, 0.4 per cent from Somalia and 0.2 per cent from Sri Lanka were considered eligible.

In Europe, governments have increasingly awarded other kinds of status to those it feels are endangered but do not qualify as Convention refugees. Often these are underpinned by international instruments such as the UN Convention against Torture – Article 3 in particular, which stipulates that no one should be returned to a state 'where there are substantial grounds for believing that he would be in danger of being subjected to torture' – and the European Convention on Human Rights, Article 3 of which states that 'no one shall be subjected to torture or to inhuman or degrading treatment or punishment.' Sometimes 'humanitarian grounds' are judged sufficient for permission to stay in a country; sometimes – as in Austria and Germany during the 1990s – asylum seekers are simply left with no status at all: they have been refused leave to remain, but to send them back would contravene Article 3 of the European Convention.

In Britain, 'exceptional leave to remain' is granted at the discretion of the Home Office. It is an inconsistent, opaque and unreliable award, and because it is discretionary, there is very little argument to be had about it. It is nonetheless a means of extending some sort of sanctuary to refugees who are refused Convention status. Although Britain withheld that status from 99.6 per cent of the Somalis who requested it in 1996, 93 per cent were given exceptional leave to remain. In practice, Convention status has tended to entail the right of permanent residence in host states. A country like Germany, heroically overextended as it is, which makes the political (and perhaps economic) calculation that it can no longer afford to offer permanent residence to large numbers of people, is free to use a 'humanitarian' alternative to the Convention to mitigate the plight of people in danger. Germany took more than 350,000 refugees from Bosnia during the war, on the understanding that they would return once conditions permitted. By late 1998, the majority had gone back – some were forcibly repatriated – and, as the Milosevic evictions began in Kosovo, it made ready for another influx – Kosovars, this time, although 150,000 or so had already entered in previous years. At the end of 1999, many people from Kosovo were also being told to return. There is something eminently practical about this approach. Yet many of those who work with refugees and asylum law see discretionary awards and other ad hoc measures as liable to weaken, rather than buttress the Convention.

Some people believe the Convention is obsolete in any case. 'The present arrangements,' Bruce Anderson wrote in the *Spectator* in 1999, 'commit us to obligations which we can never meet, so they ought to be repudiated.' He argued that an annual quota of 50 asylum seekers was a manageable intake for Britain – in a year when 71,000 fetched up – provided there were interim measures to deal with cases such as 'the plight of Jews in the 1930s, the Hungarians after the 1956 Uprising and the Ugandan Asians'. These are the bracing tones of the Right. They pinpoint one aspect of the Convention that has, indeed, become obsolete. It was drawn up as the Cold War got under way and quickly began to serve the West's purposes in the conduct of that war: it inclines, in any case, to the language of 'individual' rights and to 'political' rather than 'humanitarian' grounds for asylum. 'Political', of course, came to mean anti-Communist, which is why the Communist regimes bridled at the Convention and why, in 1965, the US amended its Immigration and Nationality Act to grant Convention status to almost anyone coming from a Communist country. In the absence of Cold War imperatives, the liberal adherence of Western signatories to the terms of the Convention is, with some exceptions, waning fast. In its place are 'temporary protection', exceptional leave to remain, 'de facto refugee' status, 'Duldung' (or 'tolerated status') and other forms of halfway house. There is less international political advantage nowadays in accommodating refugees. Far fewer of the people who wish to claim asylum are anti-Communists in any useful sense, even if they come from the remains of the Eastern bloc. As for domestic political advantage, there is none. Many asylum seekers, if they could get in, would be black; a proportion coming from the East are Roma. Most electorates in the rich world have set their hearts against that kind of influx.

The shift towards the exclusion of refugees, involving a curious mixture of 'harmonisation', under the auspices of the EU, and makeshift on the part of member states, has enormous implications for the Convention. Matters are much as Stephen Sedley predicted in 1997, when he argued that unless it is seen as a 'living thing, adopted by civilised countries for a humanitarian end, constant in motive but mutable in form, the Convention will eventually become an anachronism'. Perhaps it became an anachronism when the ideological conflict which gave it a straightforward application came to an end. In the closing years of that conflict, the means to reach a country of asylum were, like so much else, deregulated: now the market in clandestine entry is booming, as national airlines, immigration services and consular facilities shut down the official channels to sanctuary. But the commitment to provide asylum is harder to shift away from the state. Unable to put it out to tender, governments can only hope to marginalise and degrade it.

Britain has been marginalising and degrading its obligations for years. It is now a master of asylum degradation. It has one of the highest totals (as opposed to percentages) of unemployed in Europe. It is one of the continent's most urbanised countries: it can invoke 'overcrowding' to justify its position. Germany is not far behind Britain in terms of population density and Düsseldorf, its fastest growing city in the mid-1990s, expanded more rapidly than any comparable city in the UK. With 10 per cent unemployment, it has the highest jobless total in the EU. Yet it now has far more asylum seekers than Britain. It is possible, then, to sustain some form of open asylum policy, as Germany has – and

France did in the early 1930s – in the face of demographic or economic pressures. On the whole, however, if a country is opposed to immigration, it will want to underplay its asylum obligations.

Britain, which received hundreds of thousands of Jewish refugees from the Russian Pale of Settlement at the end of the 19th century, was not always a malingerer. A cursory account of the change that set in after 1900 would have to begin with the extraordinary cable sent to London in that year by Sir Alfred Milner, the British High Commissioner in South Africa, warning that a boatload of wealthy Jews masquerading as needy fugitives was bound for Britain and that 'no help should be given them on their arrival as anyone asking for it would be an impostor.' Milner's pre-emptive strike against some 350 Jewish refugees from the Anglo-Boer war was a good example of the anti-semitic chaff that had begun to confuse British public opinion on the matter. The *Cheshire* docked in Southampton amid dark suspicions that troops were being sent to South Africa to fight on behalf of Jewish finance while British Jewry was failing to support Her Majesty's war effort. The *Daily Mail* rallied to Milner's call as the exhausted passengers disembarked at Southampton and 'fought for places' on the train. 'Incredible as it may seem, the moment they were in the carriages THEY BEGAN TO GAMBLE . . . and when the Relief Committee passed by they hid their gold and fawned and whined, and, in broken English, asked for money for their train fare.'

There are several contenders for the turning point in Britain's approach to refugees, but the *Cheshire* affair is a strong one. The *Mail* enjoyed a circulation of over a million; the *Jewish Chronicle*, the strongest voice in defence of the *Cheshire* refugees, had rather fewer readers. 'Anti-alienism' had begun to cohere as a vigorous, incendiary call addressed to a large public, with governments responding accordingly, while sympathy for refugees became a muffled but powerful interstitial force, at local and national levels, in the form of voluntary organisations and support committees. How little this has changed can be seen from a headline in the *Mail* in October 1999: 'The Good Life on Asylum Alley', over an article revealing 'the shocking ease with which refugees play the benefit system'. It was left to the *Jewish Chronicle* to recall that 'similar sentiments have been expressed about numerous immigrant communities . . . over the years – including, of course, Jews.' Meanwhile, the Government stresses the importance of the 'voluntary sector' and 'community groups' in arranging housing for asylum seekers.

During the South African War the mood was starker, no doubt, than it is now, and the Aliens Act of 1905 confirmed a rampant mistrust of foreigners, which the outbreak of war in Europe only served to reinforce. Further restrictive legislation was passed in 1914; Germans were interned and deported; there were anti-German riots across many towns. Yet Britain remained ready to respond to appeals that squared with the political objectives of the day. Having guaranteed the neutrality of Belgium in 1914, for example, it reacted to the German invasion by taking in nearly a quarter of a million Belgian evacuees. Anti-alienism lost no impetus with the Armistice; by the end of the 1920s it was possible for a Labour Home Secretary, John Robert Clynes, to explain to a Jewish delegation alarmed about the precarious status of refugees that the right of asylum was not the right of an individual to obtain it but the right of 'the sovereign state' to confer it. The record of the 1920s and 1930s, which John Hope Simpson drew up in 1938, seemed to prove the point. The intake of fifteen thousand Russians – most of whom relocated to France or the Balkans – and eight or ten thousand refugees from Germany was paltry by comparison with the country's showing in the 19th century, or with the generosity of other states at the time. Simpson did not foresee that the Government would ease its entry restrictions in the months leading up to the outbreak of war – or, indeed, that it would take in about 50,000 Jewish refugees – and argued with some passion that Britain 'should show a braver record as a country of sanctuary'. More than sixty years later, with the number of asylum seekers at wartime levels, bravery is still in very short supply.

The underlying problem, Simpson believed, was 'an excessively cautious . . . immigration policy' and, in the aftermath of the Second World War, that caution only increased. The solidarities of Empire and Commonwealth, developed across racial boundaries in the course of the conflict, turned out to be provisional. The problem was straightforward. The British Ministry of Labour had characterised it in 1949 as the difficulty of 'placing . . . colonial negroes' at a time when there was a need for migrant workers – a difficulty which, the Ministry insisted, lay squarely with white employers and the rise of an informal 'colour bar'. Over the next fifty years, British immigration policy was largely shaped by the racial anxieties of voter majorities who had survived two depressions, an on-again-off-again class war and two 'world' wars. Like the newspapers they read, they were quick to foresee impending disaster and took an alarmist view of the brief disturbances in 1948 and 1949 involving Arab and African seamen in Liverpool, Deptford and Birmingham. So in the end did the Government. By the early 1950s the British public had warmed to a narrow definition of kith and kin.

Restrictive legislation tends to exacerbate migratory pressure. In the countdown to the Commonwealth Immigrants Act of 1962, the Asian and black population in Britain doubled, amid fears that a door was about to be shut. The Act also encouraged those who were in Britain on a temporary basis to opt for permanent residence. Yet, from 1963 to the end of the 1980s, a minimum of 30,000 blacks and Asians entered Britain every year – and this regular intake, layered over the immigration 'bulge' of the 'beat the ban' generation, set the terms of multiracial Britain, or the 'magpie society', as Cassandras thought of it at the time. The Act of 1962, however, was intended to keep Britain white.

The spectre of the immigrant has not receded in Britain; it has simply taken another form. The asylum seeker is now the luminous apparition at the foot of the bed. Maintaining the moderate influx of immigrants from the south and east at current levels – around 60,000 per annum – entails a burgeoning visa requirement (by January 2000, nationals of 108 countries needed visas to enter the UK) and far higher rates of refusal for prospective visitors from poorer countries. In 1997, 0.49 per cent of US citizens requesting settlement in Britain were denied entry; the figure for the Indian subcontinent was 29 per cent. In the same year, while only 0.18 per cent of Australian visitors' applications were refused, the refusal rate for Ghanaian applications was over 30 per cent. As long as migratory pressure meets with a disproportionate response of this order from a receiving country, ambitious or desperate migrants – the two are not always easy to tell apart – will consider other means of entry.

Sometimes it is the only way to pursue a livelihood.

Imagine an entrepreneur, based in Kampala, who travels regularly between East Africa, Britain and India in the course of his business. He is a buyer and shipper, bringing goods out of the rich world which would otherwise be unobtainable in the communities to whom he sells on. He is also black, which is a disadvantage for anyone stepping off a plane at Heathrow or Gatwick: on his visits to Britain, questions about the duration of his stay and what he plans to do are becoming increasingly fussy; it is taking far longer to clear Immigration. After ten years of coming and going more or less freely, he arrives in Britain and has his passport seized. He is told he can have it back when he leaves. He duly presents himself to Immigration at the end of his stay; he is given his passport, but finds that his visa has been struck through. He is told that he will not be admitted to Britain again. This was precisely the case of a Ugandan trader whose visa was cancelled in 1994, for no obvious reason, except that Immigration takes a dim view of people from Africa entering as businessmen or tourists. Immigration, he reasoned, couldn't accept that an African might be able to afford a holiday or an airline ticket – asylum seekers were a much easier category to deal with. Accordingly, on his return to Uganda, he arranged for a new passport and, on his next visit to the UK, he claimed asylum. The last thing he wanted was to be classified as a refugee, but he had a business to run and a family to support.

There is no doubt that people who are not eligible for asylum are busy trying to claim it – and the numbers may well be high. One of the clumsier deceptions has been to pose as the national of a country where there is enough civil and military disruption to increase your chances of asylum. It is not uncommon for Pakistanis to claim they are

Afghans or for Albanians to claim they are Kosovars. One case, the French police in Calais told *Libération* last year, involved 'an African trying to make out he was from Kosovo'. It happens all over Europe. Moroccans, for example, pretend to be Western Saharans in order to lodge asylum claims in Spain. In the beleaguered world of immigration officials, the presence of 'bogus' or 'abusive' asylum seekers inflames the culture of suspicion, which sooner or later extends to all applicants, plausible or not. As a result, more and more people who might be eligible for asylum are denied it. Figures in recent years – excepting the period of the Kosovo crisis – bear this out. In Britain, according to the Home Office, there were around 21,000 applications in 1997, of which 85 per cent resulted in rejections. Of the appeals against rejection heard in that year, 4400 were dismissed and 130 allowed. The rate of successful asylum applications rose towards the end of 1999, but the Home Office would still prefer to show high rates of refusal – counting the number of failures to attend for interview, for instance – since these can be used to adduce a growing problem of 'bogusness' and 'abuse'.

There are ways for governments to minimise 'asylum abuse' without abandoning the cherished goal of low immigration, but they involve more painstaking methods of verifying asylum claims, while ruling out less trigger-happy negative decisions. A resource base – something more comprehensive than a pile of US State Department or British Foreign Office reports – might be set up for the benefit of officials dealing with asylum claims. It would provide reliable information about countries and regions from which asylum seekers came, and more detailed material about the threats faced by specific groups of people in those places. It would be available not only to immigration staff dealing with claims in the first instance, but to appeals adjudicators. In the mid-1990s adjudicators throughout Britain were making an average of five daily requests for clarification on points of detail, in order to proceed to a decision. In 1996 the appeals authority had one research assistant to deal with these queries (the asylum review tribunal in Australia had over thirty).

More specialised, continuous training might be provided to the same decision makers: in asylum law, in the scope of the relevant international instruments, including the 1951 Convention, and in fundamental, face-to-face issues: an individual who has been harassed, interrogated, detained and worse by servants of the state in his country of origin may be unable to account for himself to servants of the state in a country of asylum. There are enormous pressures on immigration officials in the EU, and Britain in particular. They are asked to juggle the skills of the grief counsellor with those of the claims assessor acting for a hard-bitten insurance company; all the while, they have a wary eye on annual immigration statistics. This is a working environment in which regular policy guidelines issued by the appropriate ministry are simply not enough. Yet more thought, one suspects, has been given to training and support for police dog-handlers.

The boldest initiative would involve setting up a body of experts to assess asylum claims in the first instance. The expertise required would include first-hand knowledge of the countries and regions from which asylum seekers came, and of refugee situations overseas; clinical experience with physical and mental trauma, familiarity with international instruments such as the 1951 Convention and a working knowledge of ad hoc measures (exceptional leave to remain, 'humanitarian' status, and so on). Such a body, it might be objected, would be predisposed to find in favour of applicants. But anyone who believes in the principle of asylum has an interest in ensuring it is not debased. Whether a board of this kind were quasi-autonomous or fully independent, as it is in Canada, it would be self-regulating.

Britain is one among many wealthy countries that prefer to keep prejudice and ambiguity intact as a line of first defence against asylum seekers. In 1999 the Government recognised a need for a new body of some sort, but since the Home Office would rather discourage claims in the first place than improve the determination procedure for claimants, it chose instead to create a National Asylum Support Service. The main function of this service, which came into being in January 2000, seems to be to dispense vouchers to asylum seekers, which they can exchange for food and goods in retail outlets that agree to take them. The Government regards anything but benefit in kind 'as an incentive to economic migration', and so the asylum seeker's weekly cash allowance is limited to £10. Some local authorities had already begun to operate a voucher system after the 1996 Immigration and Asylum Act – you could see the results in supermarket queues, where cashiers, forbidden to give change, urged refugee customers to top up to the full value of the voucher with a handful of wrapped sweets, a six-pack of instant coffee sachets or a cookery magazine (cover story: 'Going Balsamic'). This, rather than people aiming for specific countries of refuge, is what we ought properly to describe as 'asylum shopping'.

The British Government has claimed that withholding cash benefits brings it into line with other countries which provide 'support in kind', but if that is desirable, why not look to the great normative model of Africa, which contains around half of the world's refugees, and simply distribute a monthly per capita allocation of oil, salt, sugar and beans? Of course, the countries Britain has in mind – Germany, the Netherlands, Belgium and Denmark – are members of the EU, and the strategy here is parity of penalisation, conceived in the hope that asylum seekers will not prefer one EU member state over another on the grounds of its being a 'soft option'.

The arguments about why asylum seekers end up in certain countries and not others are intricate. They have to do with colonial history, family connections, relays of information and, above all, with the traffickers in whose hands refugees put their lives. Social security entitlements appear to come low on the list of priorities for the survivor of an 'anti-terrorist' operation in Turkish Kurdistan who leaves his village on horseback, calls on his cousins, raises the cost of a passage to sanctuary, travels by bus and truck to Izmir or Istanbul, buys a place on a boat to Albania and, three months later, still in the hands of a trafficking network, is invited to step out of a lorry on the A3 and make his way to a police station in Guildford.

The Refugee Council in Britain always argued that the money going into the creation of the National Asylum Support Service would have been better spent on clearing Britain's backlog of unresolved asylum cases. But governments are less interested in devising a fair asylum policy than in whether or not they are seen by electorates as willing hosts to the 'scum of the earth' (the Dover Express again). By failing to address the backlog of unresolved applications or to rethink the assessment of claims in the first place, governments have compounded the situation that anti-immigrationists find so deplorable.

Britain's backlog leapt from 12,000 undecided cases in 1989 to 72,000 in 1991. There were around 100,000 at the turn of the century. Britain is not the only country with this problem – it has arisen in Canada, Australia, Sweden and the Netherlands. It is normally solved by formal or de facto amnesty, but the longer it takes to clear a backlog, the likelier it is that the system will become discredited. Once a claimant has been hung out to dry for years without a decision on his status, it no longer matters whether he is eventually refused, since the length of his stay will make it hard to deport him without a public outcry or a protracted legal battle. In practice, most of the people whose applications are finally refused after years of deliberation are unlikely ever to leave the country. This is immigration by government default.

The backlog in Britain became entrenched when the Home Office attempted to speed up its decisions on asylum claims: refusal rates soared and the appellate system was unable to cope. It is a fair guess that a proportion of those who were refused felt that they had a strong case to appeal. Swift decisions, based on a 'no immigration' agenda, are not as helpful as good decisions; and backlogs, as the Immigration Law Practitioners' Association and others have suggested, encourage 'unfounded applications for asylum', as word travels back down the line that, if rumbled, a dubious claimant will in any case remain untraceable for years. In 1997, according to one controversial estimate, there were nearly 250,000 unsuccessful asylum applicants staying on in Britain without authorisation. A country that fails to operate a fair and reasonably fast determination procedure cannot enforce a 'removals' policy – and without the possibility of removals, the entire process of asylum determination is worthless from the outset: one may as well throw everyone out or let everyone in. On the face of it, re-cent British administrations have played to the anti-immi-gration gallery with a no-nonsense posture on asylum, while in reality multiplying the grounds for its anxiety. The Labour Government's Immigration and Asylum legisla-tion, which came into effect in April 2000, indicates no change whatsoever.

Posture may well be one of the reasons asylum policy has become so degraded. As the nation-state grows harder to patrol, governments are thrown back on gesture and salesmanship. Sovereignty is an adaptable creature, and very durable, but under the new pressures of human move-ment, sovereign assertion is becoming a rictus on the phys-iognomy of nations that once wore the mask quite amenably. Even the coming and going of prosperous peo-ple between countries puts stress on their points of entry – there were 86 million arrivals in Britain in 1998 – while im-migration officials in the rich world can still be stretched to the limit by modest numbers of illegal migrants. The more freely capital and goods move around the rich world, the harder it becomes to inhibit the movement of people, with the hostility of conservative voters to foreign influx grow-ing in proportion as the ability to restrict it dwindles. In the normal way of things – that is, peaceably – the power of government to reverse this process is no greater than it was in the past, but its capacity to signal an intention, and proj-ect that signal, is far stronger.

This was not always the case. In 1916 there were riots in Fulham, a part of London plagued by poverty and housing shortages. Fulham was also a reception area for Belgian evacuees. Residents believed the Belgians were receiving higher benefits than families of British servicemen dying in the trenches. The response to the riots was a policy of compulsory conscription for Belgian males. The scrutiny of the liberal press and the influential voice of the voluntary sector would make a similar response nowadays – round-ups and mass deportations of rejected asylum seekers, for example – harder for a government to envisage, especially in peacetime, however popular it might be with certain sections of the electorate. In 1937, at the height of the Spanish Civil War, the British Government was pressured by anti-Fascist groups and charitable organisations into receiving 4000 Basque children. They were camped out on farmland in the Kent countryside. The news that Bilbao had fallen led to uproar among the children, some of whom broke camp in the hope of returning and enlisting with the Republic. Within days, the settlement had been summarily dispersed and brothers and sisters separated, as they were packed off to remote parts of England and Wales. The Vietnamese refugees who came in under the UN programme in the 1970s and 1980s were also obliged to disperse to locations designated by the British Government. One can imagine comparable action today – it has begun on a smaller scale with the dispersal of refugees – but the more brazen the government initiative (seeking to remove asylum seekers on a hijacked flight from Afghanistan, for instance), the greater the flurry of objections from the media, the voluntary organisations and the courts would be. No wonder posture is preferable to policy. Refugees are at the mercy of disabled governments with stern faces – and so is the anti-immigration voter, who regards cuts in cash hand-outs to asylum seekers as a sign that the party of power has his interests at heart. But that is all it is: a sign.

Who exactly is it intended for? In some European countries – France, and lately, Austria and Switzerland – the anti-immigration vote is significant. In Britain there are a few suspects on the extreme Right, but beyond this margin, it is hard, for the moment, to identify the cohort of stout Englishmen with a passion for chalky cliffs, white lavatory tiles and virgin brides. Perhaps they are out there. But if so, they are not being drawn on the subject of asylum seekers. In 1997, three-quarters of the respondents to a survey by the Institute for Public Policy Research agreed that 'most refugees in Britain are in need of our help and support' and only 12 per cent took the view that 'most people claiming to be refugees are not real refugees.' The minority has a keen eye on the media, and bigotry, for the media, is a more dependable story than tolerance. This all falls within the realm of signalling, which goes some way to explaining the tendency to minority appeasement in a period of government by semaphore.

More worrying conclusions about the IPPR study are reached by Tony Kushner, a historian at the University of Southampton, and Katharine Knox, a former Refugee Council officer, in *Refugees in an Age of Genocide*, a superb study of asylum in Britain, compiled largely from local historical sources. As campaigning historians, Kushner and Knox were encouraged by the IPPR survey, but dismayed by the fact that, even though only a small minority were sceptical about asylum claims, roughly 40 per cent of respondents were not prepared to disagree outright with the statement that most claims were fraudulent. They take this to prove that 'a century questioning the legitimacy of refugees has not been without a profound and cumulative impact' (an infectious cynicism, Hannah Arendt would have argued, transmitted to their grudging hosts by the regimes that first reviled them). 'Why is it,' Kushner and Knox go on to ask, 'that British governments past and present continue to pay greater attention to the hostile 12 per cent than the sympathetic 75 per cent?' The next question, perhaps, is why a government of liberal persuasion would not consider the reticent 40 per cent worth winning over – unless, of course, it was not a liberal-minded government at all.

London, in the closing weeks of 1999: walking back from my children's primary school, I see a young woman from Kosovo crossing at Prince of Wales Road and heading towards Camden Town. She walks with the privacy and haste of people in big cities, and in that much, she is no longer who she was. Instinctively I quicken my pace, to greet her, but almost at once, I find the way congested by a mob of half-recalled people and images, rowdy and difficult to negotiate. After a moment's hesitation, I give up and turn at the corner for home.

Flora was one of two sisters who had left Pristina at the end of 1998, travelled down into Albania and paid their way on a *gommone* to Italy. I met them at the Regina Pacis reception centre near Puglia a few weeks after they arrived. Even though we spoke at length – their English was quite good, and they had set their sights on London, where they had an aunt – it wasn't clear how deep the fear of persecution, or the grounds for that fear, really went with these two women. (Had they stayed another six months in Kosovo, they would have come to know it intimately.)

It struck me, on reflection, that my failure to greet Flora had to do with doubts about her claim to humanitarian status as a route out of the former Yugoslavia. A few weeks after meeting the sisters, I'd been to Kosovo and found their family. The father was a jovial chancer, bluff and hospitable; the mother was quite the opposite – a troubled person, shaken by her daughters' absence. There was another aunt whose husband, a musician with a nationalist lilt to his work, had had a rough time in prison. I gave the family news of the two sisters and some photos, which upset them. I was their guest for the best part of an evening, but again, I could never fully establish in what way the sisters had been persecuted.

A day or so later I found myself in a village west of Pristina where the KLA had ambushed a group of Serbian police. There was blood in the snow and a litter of spent cartridges. The village mosque had been wrecked. Most of the houses had already been abandoned earlier in the year, but one family had stayed, and they had paid the price of the ambush in the KLA's stead. Serbian police had dragged them to the scene of the crime and beaten them. The able-bodied man in the house had been taken away, leaving only a limping, terrified family of the very elderly or very young. There were worse scenes in Kosovo before the Nato intervention, but the memory of that particular farmstead would have crossed my mind as I saw Flora again in North London and the ghost of a moral judgment must have flickered there in passing, too. It was as though I had some model of the exemplary refugee – as though my high-mindedness would have been satisfied by the sight of the family from the abandoned village rumbling towards Camden Lock in their cart, rather than a glimpse of Flora walking along briskly and comfortably in her new guise as a Londoner. Yet who is to say what constitutes fear of persecution? After all, Flora had wanted to be a nurse, and Serbia had cleansed the public health sector of ethnic Albanian staff years ago.

There was something more petulant about my reserve, to do with the fact that refugees can be importunate people during their settling-in period. Fellow expatriates provide much in the way of support, but there are still questions, favours, conversations which any halfway generous character might properly follow up. Effort is required, however: small tasks that disrupt the rich person's love affair with his own stress. And the prospect of that disruption must have seemed tiresome – that neediness, too, no doubt. I was prone to a view of the uninvited that was no better than it had been a year earlier, when I'd leaned over the side of an Italian customs speedboat and gazed at the minuscule figures in the lunar field of the night-vision binoculars. It was even ambivalent, I am sure, on the issue of school, where I'd just left two small boys before catching sight of Flora. Dozens of children from the former Yugoslavia attend the school, along with a scattering of francophone African and Somali pupils, all of them with parents or wards who have exceptional leave to remain or Convention status. A sour parental anxiety stirs from its depths at the thought of language difficulties in the classroom and the diversion of resources to cope with them. It has no basis in fact. Much of the time it's hidden, in silent contention with the one-world equanimity of the *bien pensant* parent whose children learn about the death of the rainforests. But on bad days it will put in an appearance. It, too, is a sign of impatience with other people's needs. I have instant access, any time I like, to the mentality of the anti-asylum voter.

That mentality thrives on the idea that refugees are helping themselves to scarce resources: welfare, the public health service, accommodation paid for or provided by local government, premium space in the classroom. Mostly, we make these nervous calculations sotto voce, but in our discreet whispering and reckoning there is always an echo of the ranting public speaker in Auden's poem, 'Refugee Blues', composed in 1939, as Hitler's armies occupied Prague: 'If we let them in, they will steal our daily bread.' Yet thousands of asylum seekers rely far more on their own expatriate networks than they do on the state. Flora and her sister, for instance, were offered a choice on their arrival in Britain. They could remain in London with their aunt, in which case they would not be eligible for housing benefit, or they could move to designated accommodation in the North, where they would. They chose London; they were supported by their aunt and her husband for six months or more – enough time to find work – and then moved into a place of their own.

Where asylum seekers do claim benefits and occupy housing at public expense, there's no question that they are competing with host citizens for resources. The more deprived the area in which they settle, the fiercer the sense of that struggle is likely to be. (And dispersing refugees to the provinces in Britain seems bound to repeat the anguish of isolated Vietnamese families in the 1980s and the troubles twenty years later in Dover, where Kurdish and Kosovar refugees squared off against the local youth.) Why some poor people in deprived areas should resent the arrival of asylum seekers is obvious, even though the record of poor inner London boroughs suggests that friction is rare. Yet sufficiency of means can generate similar feelings, even among exponents of 'enterprise culture' who see unrestrained market forces as the motor of prosperous democracies, but would rather not acknowledge that these forces tend to favour freer movements of human beings.

It is clear, in any case, that the earnings and expenditure of migrants – including refugees – in host economies have exceeded the cost of accommodating them in the first place. This is the story of the United States, but it is also true of lesser economies, labouring under the pressure of change. Some of the most impoverished people to arrive in

Britain after the Second World War were the Ugandan Asians – refugees in all but name – most of whose wealth had been expropriated by Idi Amin. By the end of the century, they had established themselves as a bastion of British retail, with vantage points in finance, pharmaceuticals, engineering and property. More generally, the findings of the 1991 Census in Britain gave a useful synoptic glimpse of minority standing in terms of qualifications, job status and ownership, with a far higher proportion of Bangladeshi, Pakistani, Indian and Chinese males holding managerial posts than their white counterparts. The proportion of African, Indian and Chinese males with A-level qualifications, or their equivalent, was also higher than the proportion of whites to hold them.

Activists lobbying on behalf of refugees are familiar with figures like these. They repeat them endlessly to governments that chafe at the right of asylum. But to judge asylum seekers like other migrants on the basis of their likely contribution to an economy is to impose another qualification on the right of asylum which many refugees, permanently damaged by experiences in their countries of origin, may be unable to meet. They are not helped by book-keeper arguments about the high motivation of the new-comer. They need a more open defence, without proviso, which makes no appeal to the self-interest of host communities. The source of that defence, and increasingly of the funds that might be put at their disposal, is the voluntary sector: parish activists, support groups, money-raising bodies and registered charities – the network of well-informed, conscientious organisations that developed, in the absence of any public provision, at the turn of the last century.

One of the crucial links in the complicated route that Flora and her sister took from Pristina to London was a powerful figure in the Catholic Church. Don Cesare Lodeserto, who ran the Regina Pacis reception centre in Puglia, took care of the sisters and thousands of other clandestines by ensuring passage on through Italy. Without the centre as a first base they might well have been put in police custody or returned to Albania. Don Cesare was an absolutist. He had the absolutist temperament, like Naphta, Mann's Jewish Jesuit in *The Magic Mountain*. He was flatly opposed to book-keeper arguments and accepted any refugee or disadvantaged migrant who came his way. He also saw the determination of asylum claims as parsimonious haggling on the part of the rich world; the problem, he felt, lay deeper, in the global divide between rich and poor and the economic dependency to which the North had reduced the South. On that basis, he thought it worthless to discriminate between asylum seekers and other migrants. God was the judge of their real identity and, as a well-placed clerk of the court, Don Cesare had no doubt that God took the side of the poor. If there was a measure of disregard for the 1951 Convention in all this, Don Cesare's indifference to 'sovereignty' was greater. It was nothing to him that governments felt threatened by clandestine migration. 'The law should not defend the sovereignty of states,' he hectored his listeners. 'It should enshrine the dignity of man.'

Don Cesare's position was founded on intransigence as much as faith. He rejected almost any realistic policy to cope with rising asylum applications and other forms of migratory pressure that rich countries might envisage in the short term. But he made it possible for thousands of people with a tenuous hold on safety to look for something more durable. In doing so, he set himself against government – he had a weakness for contestation and political gamesmanship – because the interests of government were not those of the people he looked after. 'The only real help that they get,' he said with a perverse satisfaction, 'comes from this reception centre and from organised crime.' This was true. It was the centre that helped Flora and her sister obtain a short stay permit, after which they left for Milan. There, they obtained forged Italian passports and made their way through Switzerland and France to Belgium. In due course, they were sent back to France by traffickers, concealed in a lorry heading for the Channel Tunnel and put out a few hours later near the M25. They went to a service station and called their aunt in London; then they asked the cashier to phone the police.

When I finally caught up with them in London, they were loath to discuss their stay in Milan. It was obvious that the assistance they received from organised crime, as Don Cesare put it with such worldly candour, had not come their way without bitter negotiation and sexual harassment. They still thought well of their provider at Regina Pacis, part saint, part operator. From that quarter, at least, help had come with no strings attached.

The rights of EU citizens and those of asylum seekers have become major preoccupations in Europe. The two exist in a state of great tension. As a result of the Treaty of Amsterdam, which came into effect in May 1999, asylum, immigration and other 'freedom of movement' issues are now subject both to tighter judicial control and to closer European Parliamentary oversight – eventually, perhaps, they may become the object of Parliamentary legislation. In theory, this allows greater scope for redress in cases of human rights violations; it should also bring decisions about asylum procedures out of the backroom into fuller view. For the moment, however, what Amsterdam has done is to affirm that the EU regards asylum seekers and other migrants as urgent business. Urgent, above all, because the real emphasis of the Treaty is on full freedom of movement for EU citizens, and before this can be brought about, greater co-operation between the police and judiciaries of member states is required, if only because free movement for law-abiding individuals implies free movement for crime. High on the list of criminal activities targeted by the EU is 'human trafficking'.

The outline of the Treaty is hard to distinguish through the drizzle of eurodetail, but it is possible to make out some important changes. For example, non-EU citizens who are already long-term residents in member states should soon enjoy the same freedom of movement as EU citizens, so that (consistent with the Union's pledge to struggle against 'racism and xenophobia') a migrant from Bamako residing legally in Toulon would in theory be able to move to a job in Innsbruck or Banbury. But on the whole, it looks as though extending the freedom of EU citizens to long-term residents will entail restricting access for many non-EU citizens who are desperate to enter. How much worse matters will get for asylum seekers is difficult to judge, but if the EU toughens its procedures on immigration in general, no one will find it easier to claim asylum in the Union. Whether a concerted campaign against traffickers, led by Europol, succeeds or not, it will probably drive up prices for the refugees who depend on them and raise the risks of the journey. It must be obvious, after nearly two decades of Fortress Europe, that a war on traffickers involves heavy collateral damage to refugees.

EU members, meanwhile, will be trying to find a way to

'share the burden' of asylum seekers. The impetus, under-standably, comes largely from Germany. In 1992 alone, of roughly 700,000 applications in 14 European states, nearly half a million were lodged with Germany. Other countries such as Sweden and the Netherlands – and Austria, natu-rally – would also like to see a move in this direction. Bur-den-sharing is all the more pressing because the rule, agreed in the Dublin Convention in 1990, that an asylum application must be dealt with in the country of 'first ar-rival', is easy to circumvent: if the refugees at Don Cesare's centre wished to lodge their claim somewhere in Northern Europe, they were normally granted a short-term stay in Italy (20 or 30 days) which would allow them to reach a big city and negotiate the next leg of their journey. Refugees often want to go where an expatriate base is already estab-lished but, just as often, they have to take what's on offer. A client may say to a trafficker that he or she just wants to get out of a place; the trafficker will be eager to assist, but quick to add that he only does Denmark and Germany. Countries taking high numbers of refugees want compensation from other member states, and perhaps, in times of crisis, a sys-tem of sharing out numbers – regional dispersal, in other words. By 1999, plans were underway for a European refugee fund, available to states with a high intake of asy-lum seekers, but to amount to anything, it would have re-quired ten or twenty times the annual budget of the pilot fund – and a guarantee that it would not be used to shuffle asylum seekers from one country to another against their will. Beyond this, there is no consensus on burden-sharing.

The Treaty of Amsterdam empowers the EU to agree a set of 'minimum standards', not only for the way in which refugees are received and what entitlements they have, but for determining who is and who is not a refugee. At the centre of the debate, once again, is the Convention of 1951. On one side are the governments of host countries, who believe it is outdated; on the other are the support committees, refugee lawyers and NGOs, who feel that EU states will take the opportunity of 'updating' it to substitute discretionary policies for obligations. This is, in other words, a reopening, and a sharpening, of the old quarrel about right of asylum and whose it is to exercise. The Convention should have settled that. Fifty years on, however, most European signatories now want the right to confer or refuse asylum – a right they do not enjoy under the Convention, and which can only be exercised at the expense of the refugee.

The member states of the European Union do not care for the views of a radical like Don Cesare, but they recognise the great gulf, of which he spoke, between many refugees' countries of origin and the West. At the European Council's summit meeting in Finland in October 1999, the Presidency acknowledged, in effect, that asylum seekers would not be an issue in Europe if the conditions they were fleeing could be improved. An unremarkable insight. For several years now, EU institutions and advisers have been urging the organisation towards 'a greater coherence of internal and external policies', by which they mean that they would like to address the 'refugee problem' at source and that whoever has an interesting idea about how to do so should come forward. So far, the results have been disappointing. Here is the Presidency's list of 'things that need doing' in countries which generate large numbers of asylum seekers: 'combating poverty, improving living conditions and job opportunities, preventing conflicts and consolidating democratic states and ensuring respect for human rights, in particular rights of minorities, women and children.'

Less venerable bodies might have come up with the same conclusions after five minutes under the shower, but the vagueness of the language should not obscure the force of the intention: the EU is adamant that it wants to reduce the number of asylum seekers entering its territory, and if it could impose market democracy on states that produce refugees, it would. The alternative is to deploy the equivalent of an army and several flotillas along the common border, but the evidence so far is that a pristine Alpine valley, superbly patrolled, which stretches from Limerick to Vienna (and in a few years' time to the forests of Belarus, Ukraine and Lithuania) will never be impregnable.

Europe's desire to reduce the number of regimes that punish or neglect their populations is fair enough. Until it can do so, one other option remains open. It is known as 're-gionalisation'. This means trying to ensure that the bulk of the world's refugees, between 14 and 18 million in the closing years of the 20th century, remain where they are: in Africa, Asia, the fraying margins of the former Soviet Union and the Middle East. In 1999 a High Level Working Group on Immigration and Asylum, appointed by the European Council, drew up a set of 'action plans' for six of the countries generating large refugee and migrant populations. Since the idea is to reduce the flow of people into Europe, these blueprints contain a range of recommendations on fostering regional human rights and boosting development. Most are innocuous; some are useful, but none is likely to bring dictatorships to their knees. In other respects, the documents are both controversial and cynical.

A draft plan for Sri Lanka, for instance, notes that it is

'primarily a country of origin of migrants and, since 1983, of asylum seekers. The ongoing armed conflict has caused Tamils from the North and North-Eastern provinces to flee to India and further afield . . . Almost 90 per cent of all migrants from Sri Lanka are Tamils.' The draft also states that Tamils are at risk of being press-ganged into the guerrilla movement and rounded up for interrogation by the Government as suspected guerrillas. On this basis, you would expect many petitions for asylum on the part of Sri Lankans to meet the requirements of the Convention or to qualify them for 'humanitarian status'. The authors of the draft plan are more intent on finding ways to keep jeopardised Tamils inside the territory: they emphasise the success of local projects in safe areas which 'facilitate the reintegration of returnee populations' and 'strengthen the capacity of host communities to cope with influxes of displaced persons'.

The importance of protecting and providing for terrorised people in situ, with food, medicine and other forms of relief, is not in question. The danger is that this will weigh against Tamil refugees arriving in Europe. In order to pre-empt any such arrivals, the document goes on to suggest that EU countries should 'organise an information campaign' in Sri Lanka 'to warn against the consequences of illegally entering EU member states . . . and of using facilitators to gain entry to the EU'. It also advises the EU to pursue 'with the Sri Lankan authorities the possibilities of return programmes' for those who have already breached the fortress. Hovering at the edges of this thinking, without quite taking shape, is the idea that the world, or Europe anyhow, will become a more agreeable place if the global figure of refugees can be reduced by encouraging, or forcing, persecuted people to flee on a local basis only – to a neighbouring state or, indeed, from one part of their country to another. Those who take the latter course are not technically refugees, since they have not crossed their national frontier, but their lives are no better, and often worse, than they would be, had they gone into exile. At the end of the 1990s, according to the UN, the world contained around 30 million 'internally displaced persons' – double the number of refugees. The virtue of policies which add to that stock is questionable.

In Sri Lanka, like most other countries in conflict, persecution and poverty are inextricably linked. It stands to reason that some Tamils who have not faced the one will make a bid for the rich world in order to escape the other, quite likely in the guise of asylum seekers. Whether or not the authors foresaw it, the implication of the draft action plan for Sri Lanka is that an automatic screening process to distinguish refugees from economic migrants can be introduced simply by financing support programmes inside Sri Lanka to the point at which the EU deems there is adequate local protection for endangered people. From this it will follow that, persecuted or poor, or both, any Tamil who sets out for Europe must, by definition, be an economic migrant.

The same approach seems to lurk in the draft action plan for Afghanistan, which raises the possibility that some Afghan refugees are driven west by poverty rather than persecution. 'Since the economic prospects in their countries of first stay are increasingly bleak . . . they decide to move on, in particular to the EU.' They are, however, rather few in number. During the 1990s roughly 100,000 Afghans sought asylum in Europe – nearly half were rejected. Iran, Pakistan and the Central Asian Republics, in which it is proposed to 'regionalise' or, more accurately, confine Afghan refugees in future, already contain between three and four million. Burden-sharing, then, is strictly a tussle between developed countries. The real burden must remain where it originated – and with those regions there is little evidence of Europe's willingness to share anything very much.

The big questions are not addressed. How will the consent of 'regional' host countries be obtained? In Western Europe, refugees are regarded as a drain on resources: why should they not be regarded in the same way by states which are constantly exhorted to emulate the prosperous democracies? If regional hosts are reluctant to accept refugees, will the EU buy their co-operation? And if so, how will it reply to the charge that this, too, is a form of human trafficking? The plan raises the prospect of readmission agreements between EU states and Afghanistan's neighbours. But what guarantee is there that an Afghan bundled out of Europe on a flight to Pakistan, where radical Islamic groups with or without links to the Taliban are targeting secular moderates, would be safe from persecution?

In the abstract, regionalisation has much to recommend it. Exile communities remain within hailing distance of home; so does the political opposition. The affinity of the host culture with that of the refugee makes settlement less painful. Dissident 'brain drain', or transfer of expertise, from poorer regions to wealthy economies, is kept to a minimum. Yet few of these principles obtain in reality. First, refugees who can only move one door down may remain constantly in 'fear of being persecuted' – the Somali camps in Kenya have borne this out. Second, common culture is often only a result of steely management or fragile truce, its fault lines invisible to the outsider. Algeria and Yugoslavia once had the appearance of stable, consensual communities, but they are no longer places where refugees from contiguous states would feel safe; the same is true for many Afghans in Pakistan. Finally, loss of expertise may not be a net loss. Many Afghan women are Convention refugees in the US, thanks to pressure from American feminists to resettle them. There, if they choose, they can mobilise for change in Afghanistan. In the meantime, far more brutal kinds of brain drain are going on in Pakistan. The dead body of a 'regionalised' Afghan refugee on the road out of Gujrat is no use to anyone.

The 'draft action plans' will be superseded by revised plans, and revisions of the revisions, until a glut of negotiated drafts has brought the European Council to a digestive crisis. However it responds, the early versions of these plans testify to the kind of policy Europeans have in mind. They belong in the great archive of our thinking about asylum – and deserve a wider audience than they will ever get.

One of the most striking suggestions they contain is for new outposts of Fortress Europe, in the form of immigration officers stationed in the 'regions': monitors, gleaners of information, inspectors of resettlement applications – the idea is vague. It might mean no more than an extraordinary consular service: a similar post was set up by the US in Southampton at the turn of the last century to screen immigrants in transit through England. The oddity is that the new vigilance should fall to Immigration – normally within the ambit of a country's home affairs – rather than a foreign office department. This may seem trifling, but it alerts us to the disappearing distinction between inside and outside – and the speed at which nations are ceasing to be what they were.

The idea of projecting national security into the heartland of the invader is to do not with expansion but seclusion; not with the will to encounter but the will to privacy, in a world where the privacy of states and unions is a dying privilege. A redoubling of frontier control several thousand miles from the physical frontier is only conceivable when that frontier is no longer an adequate marker of interior and exterior. This is as true for the EU's common border, soon to expand to the east, as it is for the frontiers of its members. The mobility of everything they once contained and everything they once excluded, the coming and going, the constant transfer – all this friction on the cordons of sovereignty is reducing their tension. It is in the areas of slack that the game of cat and mouse between traffickers and migrants, on the one hand, and immigration officials, on the other, is played. The presence of immigration control beyond the border will add to the complexity of things, in a world of overlapping and competing jurisdictions. That is good for the game. It can only intensify.

Naturally, most citizens, like governments, believe that the outer edges of their states should be reinforced. In the wider context, however, it is not consensus within states that matters, so much as consensus across them. The members of a rich nation, or a federation, may respect its borders, yet if millions of people beyond those borders see them only as a barrier to safety or prosperity, then they are no longer a matter of consensus, but of dispute. Disputes over borders are also disputes over the extent of sovereignty; in the past they have involved secessions or rival states going to war. The new dispute sets the desire of individuals to move freely against the will of states to impede that movement. It is not a war so much as a war game, but it puts rich states on a war footing, as they go about the morose task of entrenching their frontiers – and posting scouts beyond the gates to shore up their integrity.

Meanwhile there are plenty of organisations and individuals in Europe who do not believe that refugees should pay the price for the EU's refortification. In the 1980s, Christian activists in the US revived the concept of an 'underground railway' to run thousands of refugees illegally from El Salvador through three international borders and give them sanctuary in American churches. One can imagine the legal equivalent of that process, undertaken inside Europe on behalf of asylum seekers outside the Union – a series of actions and appeals against member governments, invoking everything from domestic case law to the regional and international covenants to which states are signatories.

The drift of high-level pronouncements from the EU is that this will not be necessary: refugees will still be treated in accordance with the obligations of host states. But this is hard to take at face value, now that asylum seekers are no longer welcome in Europe without being invited – via modest resettlement programmes, a trickle of visas, and temporary admissions from countries in crisis. If they enter by other routes, they must face the consequences: first, that their primary motive for doing so will be seen as economic and, second, that the fact of illegal entry is likely to prejudice their case. For the growing list of governments who wish to keep them out, the best interpretation of the Convention Relating to the Status of Refugees can only be to run it through the shredder.

II

In Western Europe – the western Mediterranean particularly – it is impossible to follow asylum seekers without running across large numbers of 'economic migrants' who
also enter illegally, mostly from Albania, North and sub-
Saharan Africa. Unlike most of the world's migrants, they
are not well to do. Many are poor; others who may look
poor are simply run ragged, drained by the distances
they've covered.

The people I'd seen ferried from an abandoned hulk off
the coast of southern Italy in 1998 were typical: the fatigue,
and the sense of relief, were palpable. Then there was the
brusque 'Up, up' – a haunting summary of the thousands of
miles that one migrant from Sierra Leone had put behind
him. And the flip of the hand, which seemed to toss so
many questions into the air. How do you make your way
from Freetown to a dank little Italian port in winter, where
the rain is sheeting down onto the concrete quays? Had he
come across the Sahara? As a clandestine migrant from a
country at war, he might well have expected leave to remain
on humanitarian grounds. But what if he had come from
Niger or Mauritania or Nigeria? What if he had fled, not
from direct, political persecution, but from a state of affairs
so bad that it was intolerable, or even life-threatening, to
stay?

The UN High Commissioner for Refugees publishes a
handbook for signatories to the 1951 Convention, advising
on procedures and criteria for determining refugee status.
In the chapter dealing with 'Inclusion Clauses', the advice

is as follows: 'The distinction between an economic migrant and a refugee is sometimes blurred . . . Where economic measures destroy the economic existence of a particular section of the population . . . the victims may, according to the circumstances, become refugees on leaving the country.' And then, on a more cautious note: 'Objections to general economic measures are not by themselves good reason for claiming refugee status.' The intention of this passage is to circumscribe and reinforce the right of asylum by ruling out the possibility of a claim on grounds of poverty alone. But it also concedes that poverty may be a form of torment – and in broader terms, that it may often wait on persecution. The care that is taken to distinguish refugees from other, disadvantaged migrants is perfectly proper. In the meantime, there is plenty of evidence to suggest that those who try to enter the rich world by stealth in search of a livelihood are not much better off than refugees. Often they are worse off.

In the late 1990s, when the number of illegal migrants leapt in Italy, the newspapers were full of editorials about the resulting 'social and ethnic tensions'. But 'social' tension within Italy and other Western European states has far more to do with a greater geo-economic strain between the rich world and the poor world – and 'ethnic' tension is merely a variation on that theme. Forty or fifty years ago, Italians who arrived in a northern city like Milan from the south and east of the country, were mistrusted in much the same way as North Africans, Albanians and Nigerians are now. They were the ethnic migrants of their day.

Until 1961, when the Fascist 'anti-urbanisation' law was repealed, tens, perhaps hundreds of thousands of 'undocumented' persons lived and worked illegally in the north of

Italy. They were said to be noisy, or violent, or predisposed to crime, just as the Albanians and Maghrebis are now. The difference is that, by and large, Italian migrants who headed north in the 1950s and 1960s found remunerative work in a highly industrialised environment. In most of the West, this sector has shrunk. Whatever their qualifications, many of the new migrants coming off the beaches of Puglia depend in the settling-in period on piecemeal work or fragile havens in the informal sector colonised by their fellow nationals, where jobs are unpredictable and often underpaid. They also rely on the well established economy of criminal or semi-criminal activity.

Clandestine migrants or foreigners residing in Italy without proper papers become involved in passport and ID scams and, in Milan especially, many work at the sharp end of drugs and prostitution: young Albanian and Nigerian women can be pressed into service as soon as they make contact with expatriate networks. There are jobs in the North, of the kind that Italian migrants would have found in the 1960s – a number of workers in the steel furnaces of the North-East are sub-Saharan Africans – but there are fewer of them now, and the alternatives for those migrants who are drawn into criminal activity are less obvious.

The connection between crime and clandestine migration, however, may not be a result of the change in Western economies. Since the years of vigorous South-North migration in Italy, or Commonwealth migration to Britain, the service sector in the West has expanded dramatically; it has also become a source of jobs for women and minorities. Migrant self-employment and the phenomenon known as 'ethnic small business', with its many vexations – including 'self-exploitation' and the exploitation of family members – are on the increase too. At the same time, a growing number of service providers and small businesses now operate in the shadow economies of wealthy countries, where employers are ignoring the law. When clandestine immigrants find themselves embroiled with illegality after their arrival in a rich country, it is often because of the nature of the work on offer and the fact that they may still be bound to the trafficking organisations that brought them in.

Many are themselves the object of criminal or unacceptable activity. In the Netherlands, for example, most aspects of prostitution are legal, but in Amsterdam in the mid-1990s, 75 per cent of the 'window girls' were non-nationals and of these, according to the Dutch police, 80 per cent were in the country illegally. The number of women arriving from the former Eastern bloc rose sharply in the early 1990s, as did the number of men suspected of trafficking. The central problem in all this has been the ownership of the women and the appropriation of their earnings. According to one study, a Dutch prostitute earning $300 a day would normally see anything between half and two-thirds of that money; a newcomer from Ukraine, capable of earning $500 in a day, would have $25 in hand at the end of it. When a court in Brussels convicted nine members of a Nigerian prostitution network in 1997, it emerged that the women recruited had been promised asylum in order to entice them out of West Africa. They could buy their freedom from the pimping circuits in Germany, Italy and Belgium for $25,000. Indenture and debt are the crimes here – and, you could argue, insatiable demand in the marketplace. None of these is committed by the illegal migrant herself. Like most people at a disadvantage, she can only collude.

There is nonetheless an underlying difficulty to do with the spread of information, and of information technology, and the new accessibility of international travel (falling airfares, rising numbers of passengers). These put strains on restrictive immigration and perhaps, too, an onus on people to circumvent them. A satellite channel on the TV in a village café, a mobile phone in a refugee camp or, higher up the scale of prosperity, an e-mail facility in an office that depends on an electricity generator, no longer seems odd: in fact they are already clichés. It is possible to send and receive – in poorer countries, mostly to receive – in ways that have certainly foreshortened the distances between continents. But these seductive forms of abbreviation on which we congratulate ourselves are virtual, like tricks of perspective that make the horizon appear closer than it is. The real effect of digital and satellite communication is to pitch the world into a more advanced state of anomaly. A Bulgarian car worker and his Danish counterpart can purchase the same luxury item – a colour television, for instance – but the first will have to work for half a year to acquire what the second can afford after half a week on the job. Nowadays, however, the Bulgarian worker is constantly being reminded of the relative purchasing power of the Dane – and it is certain that he gives this discrepancy a good deal of thought. The father of a desperate family in Burkina Faso who decides, after three bad harvests in a row, to ride into town and negotiate a loan can watch a slimming commercial on CNN while he waits in the living-room of a prestigious uncle. He is already too familiar with anomaly to take offence at what he sees: he will think of it as a form of empty magic rather than a taunt. But market capitalism is always taunting the poor, and it now has far more scope to do so than it had in the heyday of the postwar advertising moguls.

In the least developed countries, the message of globalisation is fairly constant: stay put at all costs; help is on its way. But when the remedy takes longer to work than the doctors anticipated, the urge to get up becomes harder to resist, because globalisation heightens the contradiction between promise, which is ever-extensive, and reality, which is much as it was. If salvation keeps failing to appear over the brow of the hill, it may be time to leave the plain. The poor begin to grasp that they should follow the money, since it has failed to seek them out. Some of them take the lesson to heart.

In 1990 the UN produced a finicky but useful improvement on GDP per capita as a measure of the quality of life in any given country. The Human Development Index takes account of adult literacy, life expectancy, income levels and the average number of years a child spends in school. The results are not so much profiles of countries as silhouettes, projected against a twilight of statistics. In the human development ratings compiled by the UN, 56 countries could be said to enjoy a good quality of life. The remainder are caught in the slough of middling to low. In the top 80 countries, which include Belarus, Macedonia, Jamaica and Peru, there are no entries whatever from sub-Saharan Africa – not even South Africa, the jewel in the continent's crown.

There is another, quite complex barometer of comparative wealth known as the PPP (or 'purchasing power parity') index, a measure of the relative ability of the world's inhabitants to pay for goods and services. It is derived by adjusting exchange rates to take account of cost of living differences, which are calculated, in turn, on the variable price of those goods and services across the globe. A rough hierarchy of national purchasing power can be obtained by running the per capita GDP of every country through the adjusted exchange rate. The result is expressed in a point system, with the US citizen scoring 100 points, the Luxembourgeois 116.1 and, at the *bas fonds* of the index, the farmer in Myanmar fewer than 5. Of the 20 entries at the bottom of the PPP list, 15 are sub-Saharan. In terms of the Human Development Index and PPP, globalisation in Africa is a busted flush.

Why, then, are there so few sub-Saharan hands gripping the portcullis? By comparison with Asia and Eastern Europe, Africa is a modest source of legal and clandestine migrants to the rich world, despite the strength of old colonial ties to several EU countries. It is thought that fewer than four million sub-Saharan Africans live outside the continent, although in the EU alone, there are 17 million immigrants. Part of the reason is the lure of South Africa, which drew on a vast pool of migratory labour from neighbouring states under apartheid and remains a magnet for continental expatriates, who now come from further afield and work in many different areas of the economy, including a sizeable drugs trade. Some of the biggest intakes since the early 1990s have been from Nigeria and the former Zaire.

The African case raises one of the great conundrums facing governments that want to keep out migrants from poorer countries, for it suggests that high levels of immiseration such as Africa has endured since the 1970s are not the decisive cause of migration to the rich world. It is true that many clandestine migrants are driven by poverty, but there are also many whose levels of wealth and whose quality of life are the very factors that enable them to leave. Wealthy states – EU member states, for instance – who hope to discourage migration from very poor parts of the world by a cautious transfer of resources (more advantageous bilateral trade deals, deeper debt relief and so on) should not be downcast if they discover, after a few years, that these ini-

85

tiatives have failed to improve conditions in their target countries. For a country that did indeed show an increase in GDP, adult literacy and life expectancy – a general improvement all round – would be likely to produce even more aspiring migrants than a country trying to cope with live burial at the bottom of the world economy.

For 30 years or more, Mexico was the most obvious case of the rapid growth/high sender economy. Today the model would be Korea, or Taiwan. But the broad thrust of modern migration, away from rural areas to sprawling conurbations, holds true for almost any developing country. When an agricultural revolution tears through the patterns of subsistence farming, the dispossessed are not the only people driven to the city. The beneficiaries of surplus make their way there too, buying into education and new skills: the potential for mobility, unleashed in the villages, carries well beyond the national capital.

The problem for rich nations aiming at minimal immigration from poorer countries is obvious: in attempting to discourage migration by enriching source countries, they can never rule out the possibility that they are stimulating the very phenomenon they wished to depress. In the past, a government's immigration policy amounted to a yes or a no, according to its needs and wishes, and the ability to enforce its word at its frontiers. Nowadays, it involves byzantine projections that take into account the likely effect, in terms of migratory pressure, of one region being enriched or another impoverished, and complex bilateral negotiations with source countries over migrant quotas. All the while, governments strenuously resist the conclusion about the free movement of people that they reached with equanimity about the free movement of capital: that it may be an expensive waste of time to try to fend it off.

Nobody is sure what a liberalisation of human movement would look like, any more than we could be certain in the 1980s what the deregulation of world markets would entail. Would the consequences of human beings moving around more freely than they do now turn out to be just as momentous? And would the old mechanisms of power persist in some form that left the rich world with a controlling interest in who went where (or who didn't), much as the corporate establishments of the old order were able to safeguard their ascendancy during and after deregulation?

The answers to these questions are deferred – indeed, they are difficult even to sketch out – for as long as developed countries are wedded to restrictive immigration. If they could conceive of a world in which movement was freer than it is, they might find it easier to resolve some of the more pressing problems that accompany restriction on movement now. The most obvious of these is that it becomes costlier and more of a nuisance to maintain when even a handful of aspiring migrants in poorer countries – whether they are in the process of becoming richer or not – cease to respect the borders of wealthier ones. Another is that restriction tends to encourage migrants who want real freedom of movement – which is to say, the legal right to enter and leave at their leisure – to opt for settlement or some form of long-term residency. To enter a country with a strict immigration policy, often after a good deal of paperwork and a large financial outlay, is to feel a nagging fear that next time it could all be harder; that access, which in a perfect world would be available on demand, could be cut off at any time by a surge of anti-immigration feeling or a new round of restrictive legislation.

Only those who are persecuted or cut to the quick by

poverty want to uproot permanently and fight for their place in a society where they are unwelcome. Others would sooner have the right to come and go. Europe is far from establishing any such right. In its absence, immigrants arriving from poorer countries in the last fifty years have decided, after due consideration, that the best course of action is to dig in.

It is one thing for an immigrant to take up the burden of exile for the duration of his working life and another for an entrepreneur to be fly in and fly out as he pleases; to buy goods and ship them home, install them or sell them on, and build up a business that requires more frequent visits to the rich world, more substantial purchases. Restrictive immigration tends to deny the short-term visitor the ability to spend directly in the shopping malls of Europe, to drink at the fountain of the great consumer democracies which claim to confer citizenship on anyone with the power to buy. The West prefers foreign consumers to purchase at one remove, normally through the costly mediation of Western agents and middlemen. It also favours expanding foreign outlets and international franchising. That is the way to secure more of the takings: prudence is the loyal servant of order and seclusion. Yet even if the piecemeal enrichment of poorer groups of people by bigger remittances and freer access were to stimulate migratory pressure on the West, it is not certain that the new ambition would be to settle in the rich world.

In *A Seventh Man* (1975), John Berger described the vicissitudes of clandestine migration from Portugal through Spain into France. The traffickers charged $350 per person, about a year's earnings for a peasant farmer when migration from Portugal was still illegal. Often, they cheated their clients by abandoning them in the mountains across the Spanish frontier. The migrants devised a system to guard against this:

> Before leaving they had their photographs taken. They tore the photograph in half, giving one half to their 'guide' and keeping the other for themselves. When they reached France they sent half of the photograph back to their family in Portugal to show that they had been safely escorted across the frontiers; the 'guide' came to the family with his half of the photograph to prove that it was he who had escorted them, and it was only then that the family paid the $350.

There are similar arrangements now. Families in China pay the agents' fees in instalments. They keep to the schedule only when a clandestine émigré has confirmed his safe arrival in Britain, where he, too, can make a contribution – the cost is in the region of £15,000 and rising – but failure to pay can lead to the victimisation or disappearance of the migrant. What Berger's account of Portuguese clandestines has in common with many stories today is the importance, to those who remain behind, of sending out a relative who can shore up the family economy with earnings and establish a base, of which other family members may one day take advantage.

Migrants from Africa, the Middle East and the remains of the Eastern bloc are foragers, an advance guard, illustrious adventurers – potential earners above all. They also act as intermediaries between two worlds. In the North, by their example, they vouch for the rigorous 19th-century logic of 'amelioration' and, in setting their hands to anything, offer an adaptationist lesson in endurance and versatility. They find a rapt audience – captive, in fact – in their countries of origin, whom they regale with tales of sumptuous indulgence and untold risk. But there are also long interludes of realism. By reporting back, or visiting, or returning for good after five, ten, fifteen years, migrants reinforce the scepticism of poorer, sedentary communities about the footling self-portraiture which the rich world disseminates by means of satellite television – advertising especially. In all this, it is not a picture of themselves that migrants complete by supplying the missing part, but a picture of the world beyond the village or the township. They can paraphrase, gloss and interpret the *ad infinitum* ramblings of satellite transmission and insist that the land of riches may be bleak and unforgiving, despite its advantages. As more migrants arrive in Western Europe, the demystification of the rich world gains ground. Those who enter now have fewer illusions than their predecessors, who would often rather they did not follow in their footsteps. Their successors will have fewer still, but they will keep wanting to come.

Sustaining the remittance, rolling access to foreign income across two generations, extending it, seeing it through – these are powerful motives for migrants, even though they are now less welcome in the countries where they can earn a living. In the early 1990s, when the IMF reviewed the global value of remittances, it estimated that migrants had transferred $65 billion out of their host countries in 1989; this figure exceeded by about $20 billion all official development assistance from donor states to qualifying countries in the same year. For families in a country like Tunisia, to which workers abroad now remit well over $600 million a year, or Haiti – in the region of $100 million – earners posted overseas for long periods are crucial.

*

If freedom of movement is a 'human right', as some argue, there must also be a case for the rights of communities to oppose what they do not want, including immigration. A community that successfully defeats a proposal for a local nuclear reactor is safer, by a margin, if it is built three hundred miles away instead. That is some kind of victory. Similarly, if it deflects the motorway, or defeats staff cutbacks in its hospital or a plan to bus in children from other neighbourhoods to its schools, it is ensuring that things go on as they did. Victory here, too. The adverse effect on other communities will, of course, have negative repercussions on the one whose strength of feeling spared it the brunt of the difficulty: no parish is an island. But restricting immigration may not even amount to a parochial victory.

The reason for this is connected with population growth and the tendency of poorer people to invest in kind – that is to say, in even greater numbers of poorer people, via the low-outlay strategy of having children. The restriction of migration to the rich world not only slows up the transfer of resources from rich to poor, and hampers the stewardship of local resources in poorer countries: it encourages higher rates of population growth in the world as a whole. With a net population increase of more than 80 million people a year, this is not a welcome situation, even for communities whose own populations are in decline. In one account, the poor will begin to congregate at the gates in far higher numbers than they do already.

This possibility is set out in *The Lugano Report*, a serio-comic investigation by Susan George, in which she imagines the findings of a panel of experts, commissioned by wealthy 'masters of the universe' to examine how best to keep global capitalism 'ticking over' to their advantage. The panel is dismayed by high population growth in poorer countries and the sluggish pace of wealth transfers from North to South. It foresees a huge increase in migratory pressure on the rich world. Migrant groups 'which Northern states already find difficult to assimilate into their mainstream, represent a mere fraction of those who will seek to migrate in future, as recurrent and widespread political economic and ecological breakdowns strike their own societies'.

The alarmist tone is deliberate – designed to point up the worst fears of wealthy states. But we know that at present only a very small proportion of the world's population migrate between continents: the remainder are immobile, listless even. By contrast, the panel's conclusions about the stress to which rising numbers of people subject the environment, based on projections of a world population increase from 6 billion at the millennium to anything between 8 and 12 billion by 2050, are depressingly familiar: 'mass deforestation, species habitat destruction, mushrooming, unliveable and polluted cities, lakes and seas dead from industrial and human wastes; all constantly intensified by ever-growing multitudes', the 'substance of the earth . . . consumed' – and so on.

This throws a darker, less fantastic shadow over Europe's idyll of seclusion. We know for a fact that increasing numbers of displaced people in poorer countries are 'environmental' refugees – people who are forced to abandon their homes because of a metropolitan hunger for fossil fuels, minerals, hardwoods, water and processed meat. We also know that the world's poorer communities become more numerous until their living standards improve, along with the spread of education and wider margins of choice, particularly for women of child-bearing age. Such improvements may raise their contribution to atmospheric pollution, global warming and every other item on the list of devastation – but no serious environmentalist advocates the villain's default option, of ensuring that even if the poor increase their numbers, they remain too abject to consume and pollute with the ferocity of a country like the US. Those who believe that the most urgent business now is the race against environmental depletion might reflect on liberal immigration as a way to win it. To insulate the rich world against the poor migrant is simply to fail at one of the early hurdles in the race – improvement in living standards in underdeveloped countries – and sooner or later to take the consequences. For the future of the Alpine valley, whatever its collective sensibilities and however keen its antipathy towards people of another colour or culture, the absence of non-Europeans in the cheerful micro-ecology of 'l'espace européen' has far more alarming implications than their presence.

The impending shortage of young people in a marketplace that has aimed to capture and consume the young by fattening them up into gainful consumers is also a cause for concern. Most population projections for Western Europe forecast rising numbers of elderly and falling numbers of young people – a witch's cage without Hansel and Gretel. This may account for the extremes of anger and dismay with which the West greets the arrival of 'unaccompanied minors': children from a poor or dangerous country who set out under their own steam for a richer, more stable destination, or who are sent by worried relatives and dumped, normally without any adult to ensure their safe arrival. In these powerful symbolic figures the rich world discerns the hazy demographic issues at the back of migration and begins to understand that youth and age are no longer about time, so much as space. Life expectancy in many parts of the developing world is on the increase; in others, it will remain low. But in Europe, since 1945, old age has become one of the certainties of youth. When a ten-year-old girl from Togo is hoisted over the border fence of a Mediterranean outpost of Spanish Africa and left for police patrols to find, or half a dozen Ethiopian children are discovered huddling somewhere in Arrivals at Heathrow Airport, or the miraculous survivor of a flight in the undercarriage of an Air Afrique carrier from Senegal claims asylum in France, an extraordinary confrontation takes place between a world defined largely by an excess of young people and another by a deficit.

In its distress at the arrival of unaccompanied minors, the rich world looks busily beyond them in search of someone to blame: the people who put them up to it – parents or relatives, traffickers acting on their behalf, ruthless opportunists with no notion of decency. The real transgressors, however, are the uninvited children themselves, crossing the forbidden boundary between two worlds that resemble enchanted domains in a myth of primal sundering. In the first, there is only eternal youth, endlessly extinguished and replaced; here the young seem to have swallowed up the aged. In the second, crowds of mature adults and elderly extend the limits of longevity, deferring the moment of death, unwilling to cross the threshold but unable to return and regenerate the landscape over which they hastened; here the old have begun to devour the young. The youthful intruder in the sanctuary of age is a reminder that the child is no longer father to the man. In one place, the child reproduces himself on a treadmill of infirmity and social upheaval; in another, the father reproduces himself in the desolate embrace of technology.

That globalisation has failed to coax or bully these two worlds into closer relation was the drift of a letter found in the landing gear of an Airbus that flew out of Guinea-Conakry in the summer of 1999. It was recovered in Brussels from the wheel enclosure under the starboard wing of the aircraft, along with the remains of two young Africans who had stowed away in the hope of migrating to Europe. In the letter, addressed to 'Messrs the members and leaders of Europe', the two boys, Yaguine Koita and Fodé Tounkara, explained what had led them to make a bid for the rich world: they were fugitives from the misfortune of happening to be African. The letter talks mostly of Africa and Africans – the words occur nine or ten times, the name of their own country only twice. Perhaps they made the astute assumption that no one in Europe would know where Guinea was. Or perhaps they felt strongly that their impasse in the shantics of Conakry was shared by millions of sub-Saharans. In their last will and testament, the two boys appeal to Europe's 'sense of solidarity and kindness . . . Help us, we suffer too much in Africa, help us.' They nominate 'war, sickness, food' as the great 'problems' of Africa and lament the state of African schools. The overriding motive for their departure was to risk everything for an education. 'We want to study and we ask you to help us to study to be like you in Africa.' They hid in the allotments at the near end of the airport runway and waited while a Sabena carrier taxied towards them. As it swung around to line up for take-off, they leapt the airport fence, sprinted under the howling turbines and clambered into the undercarriage. It is unusual to survive for very long at minus forty or fifty centigrade. Yaguine Koita and Fodé Tounkara died like polar explorers in some terrifying ether icefield.

In Belgium, life expectancy is nearly double that of

Guinea. Belgium has the fourth oldest population in the world; in Guinea, nearly half the population is under 15. In Belgium about 10 children are born for every 1000 head of population; in Guinea, about four times that number, although about 12 per cent die in infancy. By 2015 Belgium will have one of the slowest growing populations in the world – indeed, it will show a negative growth rate of -0.05 per cent; the population of Guinea will continue to grow at anything between 2 and 4 per cent.

Confidence in longevity is now normal in the West; it is a sign that we can still venerate old age, but it is a kind of avarice, too, although less fierce than our attachment to money, and it may just be that a redistribution of age and youth is more attainable than the worldwide cornucopia that globalisation is always promising to lay before the eyes of an astonished and grateful public. In North America, Australia and Europe, not only is the natural increase in population slowing up, but the foreign share of total births – always higher, proportionately, than the ratio of foreign to indigenous nationals – shows no sign of reversing the trend. In wealthy countries, neither immigration nor higher numbers of births among naturalised foreigners or non-nationals can compensate for the imminent shortage of young people.

Older people, we are told, will no longer be able to live in the manner to which they are accustomed. 'Very high volumes of migration would be needed,' the OECD believes, 'to change the trend in ageing populations' in prosperous countries. The analogy might be a basin of water with the plug out and the tap running. The first gurgling sounds are audible from 2010 onwards, when the prevailing ratio of citizens between the ages of 15 and 64 to citizens aged 65 or over is no longer sustainable: the shortfall in the first group is so large that, by 2020, nearly 80 million people will be required to restore the ratio in the US, Australia and the UK. Where should they come from, if not from the places where old age was struck off the slate in the last four decades of the 20th century?

But the rich world is unlikely to draw migrant labour from the very poorest countries – from Guinea, for example. It will look to sources closer to home (the first big supplier of migrant labour to industrialised Germany in the 1950s was Italy; it was followed by Spain and Greece, Turkey, Morocco, Portugal, Tunisia and Yugoslavia). It will also look to parts of the world with the modicum of social and economic infrastructure that many European possessions enjoyed on the eve of decolonisation. Above all, to places in which it has become embroiled by trade and the prospect of cultural penetration. A country like Australia, which touts for sales in overseas markets, with a strong emphasis on its further education opportunities, can expect high intakes of students from Asia – there were about 100,000 a year in the 1990s – many of whom will apply to remain. A country like the US that opts for massive market expansion in the East and fights two wars there for good measure will also experience migratory pressure from new sources: by 1990 there were around ten million 'Asian Americans' in the US. The poor of sub-Saharan Africa fail on all these counts.

More prosperous regions may not be so lucky either. The projected need for high numbers of immigrants is based on the notion that the economies of the rich world will continue to function in more or less the same way in the next three decades as they did in the last two. But a 25-year forecast in

Britain or Germany that ventured as much in the mid-1970s would have been debatable by the end of the century. One which envisaged continuing primary immigration into Western Europe for a further three decades on the basis of the intakes begun in the 1950s would simply have been wrong: within 20 years a combination of lower birth rates and higher living standards had produced a significant decline in Southern European emigration. In the early 1970s, meanwhile, Britain and West Germany put a stop to recruitment from further afield.

Even with zero primary migration from poorer countries, Britain and West Germany continued to receive thousands of immigrants on grounds of family reunion, and the chain of movement set up by the first phase of recruitment survived the about-turn in host country policies. In Germany especially, returning the returnable worker became less straightforward, as foreign labour was drawn into the complex web of civil society. Employers' priorities often ran counter to the policy of rotation; so did the views of trade unions, solidarity organisations, journalists and immigration lawyers. When Germany ended long-term labour intakes from Turkey there were around a million Turkish residents in the country. By the early 1980s the figure was closer to 1.6 million. Many West Germans would have been happier with none at all.

The other fear that seeped into Europe as it prepared to close down primary immigration was social division along ethnic lines: fear of the ghetto, racial segregation, a resurgence of xenophobia. In the dark days of the *gastarbeiter*, full citizenship in Germany was conferred by genealogy. Blood circulates, immigrants rotate. A German was a German wherever he or she might be; a non-German, on the other hand, was a visitor who would in due course leave and be replaced. Or not, depending on the demand for labour. West German citizenship law was haunted by the postwar break-up of Germany and by the large numbers of Germans in the Communist East. A democratic fusion of the *corps morcelé* became the ideal, for conservatives and liberals. The conservative view of the non-German resident's status was deeply defensive. But in the liberal view, too, there were grounds for caution: the recent past had tarnished the very idea of the nation-state, and with it, that of 'national' citizenship – above all, German national citizenship. To bestow it on immigrants as a privilege seemed hypocritical and perverse.

The result, however, was not the open-ended republicanism – 'relaxed coexistence', in the idiom of the Social Democrats – that West Germany had hoped for. In the early years, guest workers were capsuled from the rest of society in overcrowded living-quarters doing jobs that the indigenous population would not consider; the unavailability of citizenship for long-term residents and their children reinforced their otherness, while many of the rights they shared with Germans failed to protect them from hostility and outright attack. The loose-fitting garment that the Constitution had in mind for them turned out to be a corset.

Since May 1999, German citizenship has become easier for foreigners to obtain, but the sense of immigration as an ambiguous experiment which, once begun, could never be done with, remains strong. Within a year of the changes in the nationality law, the General Secretary of Germany's Liberal Party called for the abolition of 'individual' right of asylum – a call, in effect, for default from the 1951 Convention – on the grounds that it was 'an invitation to abuse and to unrestricted and unregulated immigration'. The Federal

Minister of the Interior, Otto Schily, had already made a cursory division of sheep and goats a few days earlier, when he told the *Berliner Zeitung* that only 3 per cent of asylum seekers were 'genuine'. Long after both men have retired into obscurity, there will be others who say much the same. At the root of their ill temper is the knowledge that asylum obligations and broader migratory pressures force governments into areas they cannot control. To inhibit immigration in one way is to encourage it in others. To deny it altogether, as Europe is now trying to do, is simply to invite a growing disregard for the law.

The mechanical paradigm of migration on which we still rely – 'push' in the migrant's place of origin, 'pull' in his destination – derives from the pioneering work of the geographer and statistician, Ernst Georg Ravenstein, on the results of the United Kingdom census of 1871. This model, with its two basic terms, has done sterling service for over a century. It has also undergone endless refinements by demographers. To apply to the present migration crisis – a crisis of perception, as our politicians would say – it requires two further add-ons. Both would address the odd effects that result from states attempting to regulate migration – and both are connected with the ideal of low immigration from poorer countries. The first might be thought of as 'reversal'. In its most unattractive form, it is based on the desperate belief that the way to do away with unwanted immigrants is to pour development aid into countries that produce them. The hope is that the narrative of immigration could be told differently and the socio-economic landscape quickly made over. The desired effect is a rewind of migrant influx, as large numbers of non-European males begin to retreat, heels first, towards the platform exits on the concourse of Cologne station and others totter backwards at high speed up the gangways in Marseilles and Southampton.

Yet, with the right spin, 'reversal' can also be a progressive idea. It involves rethinking the economic relationship between richer and poorer countries and insisting, at the tables of the World Trade Organisation, the IMF, the World Bank and the bilateral lenders, on further, deeper debt relief, faster decartelisation of wealthy producers and more prodigal overseas aid. Advocates of liberal immigration are, in some sense, only advocates of development. Yet the real protagonist of development, they argue, is the migrant: governments must study this dedicated ferryman of aspiration and reward, and then decide how to assist him in the endless business of transfer in which he is engaged.

Immigrants have always had their own co-operative associations; often they pool their earnings: they know better than anyone the needs of the communities they have come from. 'Reversal' urges high incentives – tax relief, matching funding, low interest loans – to encourage the return of capital and skills to developing countries. Such policies, the argument runs, would enable a group of immigrants in Europe who were saving to build a school or a clinic in their place of origin to raise the money far more quickly. 'Reversal' also hopes to generate the equivalent of 'sender-country pull': it advocates import tax relief in poorer countries, the creation of foreign currency accounts with attractive interest rates and the eligibility of returnees to the same benefit entitlements, where they exist, as other nationals. In this model, the immigrant is a stakeholder in two worlds – 'the natural link' between North and South and the mediating agent of a process now known in France as 'co-development'.

The liberal immigration lobby, which looks on migration as a 'transitional demand' in an unfair world, believes that the more of these agents there are, the likelier the chances of achieving parity, or painless alignment, between global rich and global poor. It argues for more intensive short-term migration, more detailed matching of supply and demand, often at local levels, which would then be rubber-stamped at the national level. Crucially, enlightened 'reversal' raises the possibility of getting migrants out again, as well as letting them in – a far less dismal prospect than the moated castle of affluence, and one which distinguishes its proponents from the cruder enthusiasts of down-payment repatriation, who would happily stuff a few thousand francs in the back pocket of an Algerian immigrant if they knew they'd seen the last of him.

Migration is a harsh process, sometimes frankly cruel, and it has always involved quite savage forms of triage, especially when it is compulsory. One has only to think of the high numbers of slave deaths in the Atlantic passage, or of the Chinese contract labour requisitioned by the New World in the latter part of the 19th century to compensate for the abolition of slavery. About half a million Chinese are thought to have embarked at Canton for Cuba and Peru between 1845 and 1900. Many were sold at auction when they arrived. The journey, via the Cape, took four or five months, during which 12 to 15 per cent of the passengers died. On a lesser scale, there are plentiful instances of suffering now. In November 1999, 14 stowaways on a 12,000-tonne ferry from Greece to Italy – most of them Iraqi Kurds – were asphyxiated when a fire broke out in one of the garages. Every few months, landmines along the Greek border with Turkey kill or maim asylum seekers from Iraq. No one knows how many illegal migrants setting out on small boats from Morocco have drowned in the Gibraltar Straits, but no one doubts a figure in the thousands.

To the clandestine migrant, however, the idea that the border may be permeable is more important than the idea that it may not be. For reluctant host states, the reverse is true. This stubborn dialectic ensures that migration remains as difficult as it always was for poorer people – and forces millions of them through an informal selection procedure, which will continue until there is no such thing as a gap in the border, an illegal migrant or a human trafficker. As another new element in the migration paradigm, it could be called 'sieving'. Its effect is, first, to separate the unfit from the fit, and then, among the fit, to recast any residual weakness as something adaptable and supple, with a high tolerance for extremes. By making it so hard for non-white contenders, the West is creating an acceptable species of foreign migrant. Nowhere is this more obvious than in North Africa.

A short man with a good car who knew everybody's business drove me over the border into Morocco. He missed the southerly road to Tetouan by a long chalk. We'd been due to make a stop there, but within an hour or two we were cruising through the outskirts of Tangier. It was a shaky start for a person who claimed to know so much. The idea was to meet a boatman, someone who ferried people across the straits to Spain for money. There was a long wait and a brisk walk up through a busy part of the city to a teahouse where the patrons sat flicking beads in front of a European Champions' League match on the house TV. Our trafficker was charming enough – he had good-humoured, rheumy eyes and spoke passable English. The two men went back some way and, even though my guide leaned on his old acquaintance, he would not be drawn on the subject of his work. He was getting on now, and looked askance at everything about his younger days. The most he would admit to were occasional deliveries of kif and hashish to Algeciras. He struck me as a waste of time.

Even so, the old boy's name turned out to have a certain currency. A few days later, when I mentioned it in passing to another smuggler, I was rewarded with a brief glimpse into the business of trafficking from Morocco. Hassan was 22 and came from Fez. He contracted boats to run drugs across the water; sometimes he delivered them himself. He was a laid-back, ambitious young entrepreneur with no interest in human cargo. He had met our man in Tangier and assured me he still took clandestine migrants over the straits. 'He won't say so now,' Hassan told me. 'No one will say it.' The business had fallen into disrepute – too many deaths, too much black propaganda from Europe. 'I ask you this simple question: how, under such conditions, can a man be proud of what he does?'

Hassan had no quarrel with migrant-trafficking, but it was easier and more rewarding to run drugs. He explained that by and large drugs and migrants were handled by separate organisations – and drugs were incomparably better business. Fifteen passengers or more on a fishing smack, paying $1300 each, cannot match the earnings of a drugs run. In two nights' good work an organisation handling drugs can recoup more than the transit value of everything the Guardia Civil confiscates in a year. With drugs, there isn't the problem of keeping people in safe houses near the beaches for days on end and arguing down to the last dirham with every customer. If things go wrong for a migrants' agent, he can't heave his passengers overboard as you would a consignment of drugs. If they go badly wrong, he has other deaths to consider, along with his own, in the final prayer. 'I know your friend in Tangier,' Hassan concluded. 'And I know his business for a fact.'

Many of the illegal migrants from Morocco make their way up to the coast from poorer villages in the south. The traffickers' fees are well above average annual earnings: they represent years of family thrift and, often enough, a family debt. It is not so much the shortage of money in Morocco that impels migration – though this is acute enough for most – as the lack of schooling and medical and legal provision: access to doctors, lawyers, decent schools is prohibitively expensive for most Moroccans. But if misfortune comes between the family and their migrant – if he is repatriated, for example, or drowned – matters are very much worse than they were before they parted with their money. About 1700 Moroccans were apprehended entering Spain illegally through Algeciras in 1997 and more than 2000 in 1998. Each one represents a family setback in Morocco.

Illegal entry from the Maghreb into Spain is modest beside the flurry of human movement, most of it legal, that has begun to blur the boundaries of Mediterranean Europe and North Africa. During 1997 three million Moroccans and Europeans passed through the tiny Spanish enclave of Ceuta, tucked into the Moroccan littoral. By 1999, the figure had risen beyond five million. Millions also travel to and from Tangier. A good proportion are registered seasonal labourers in Spain's agricultural sector – an indispensable migrant workforce – while others make their way down through France in the summer, in cars and kombis loaded with goods, and back again in September for the rentrée. With the ferry monopoly in the Straits long gone, competitive prices and several passages daily, rates of movement are likely to increase. The waters that separate the shores of the western Maghreb and southern Spain now resemble what they were before the rise of nation-states and machine-age empires: a transit point, rather than a barrier, between Africa and the Iberian peninsular.

The Mediterranean is also an objective for poorer sub-Saharan migrants. Some hope to claim asylum in Europe, but the great majority are looking for a livelihood. Most travel north along the arduous routes from West Africa – so far, no more than a few thousand every year – but here, the phenomenon of migration from poor countries is at its most simple and stark. Poverty, frustration and danger are the main motives for leaving. It nonetheless takes a particular cast of character, and a will to reach Europe – forged, perhaps, by a combination of anger and the burning wish for release – to make the journey. Those who do so are going about migration very differently from the millions of Africans who move to neighbouring states or the hundreds of thousands of others – prosperous people – who fly in and out of Europe and the US without any problem.

Year after year, African commentators, World Bank officials, foreign news editors and aid agencies wet a finger and raise it in the hope of detecting a new wind of change on the continent. There are always signs of improvement; it's a matter of looking for them. But there are still some seven million refugees in Africa and many more displaced inside their own countries. Persecution, war and injustice remain the handmaidens of post-colonial politics in much of the continent. Privation, too, is a gnawing extremity. It is a common misconception that the very few illegal migrants who make it out of sub-Saharan Africa are no better off than those who stay. Traffickers' fees and other costs can run into hundreds of dollars, which proves the existence of money somewhere in the family of a typical 'illegal' heading for the rich world. Yet the destitute too can get to Europe, on loans, or charity, or sheer ingenuity. Both the poor and the not so poor have made the cold calculation that matters may only get worse if they remain where they are. A young father knows that, if he does not die before his time, he may well outlive his own children; another sees the painstaking work of generations wilting in a dustbowl of mismanagement and corruption. Whether it is a threat or already a reality, ruin is what hounds the sub-Saharan migrant up through the desert.

For West Africans heading north, there is a 'left side' and a 'right side' – or so it appears. The fulcrum is somewhere in Niger. The easterly route takes them up through Libya, and they may find themselves on the coasts of Lebanon or Turkey before they set foot in Europe. The itineraries and transactions are obscure, but it may be that Turkish traffickers set up the last stage of the journey. They could, for example, ferry migrants to a large boat at anchor off Izmir, which is slowly filling up with other clients – typically Kurds – and then head west into European waters to decant them into smaller vessels. This, perhaps, was the way that the men from Sierra Leone had come – a fantastically roundabout way – before I saw them brought off the old hulk in Santa Maria di Leuca.

The 'left side', or westerly route, involves a journey through Algeria, Morocco and often the two Spanish seaboard enclaves of Ceuta and Melilla, remnants of Spain's imperial holdings in Africa. The demise of this modest empire, at the time of Franco's death, led to the creation of what is now one of the oldest refugee encampments in the world, as the inhabitants of Spanish Sahara fled Moroccan annexation and settled in Algeria. About 250,000 Saharans are still waiting in the Algerian camps for an opportunity to return. Spain has managed to parry Moroccan designs on Ceuta and Melilla, however, and so, on its entry into the European Community in 1986, two forward posts of the future Union came into existence on the continent of Africa.

Ceuta is no more than 20 square kilometres, with a population of 75,000. It is modern, artificially and lavishly developed in parts by mainland subsidies, and unmistakably a garrison community with a high proportion of Army personnel. As EU territory in Africa, it is another of Europe's frontline defences against migrant intrusion. It also provides for those whom it has failed to intercept at the Moroccan border, settling them provisionally in a large camp and eventually processing them into work and liberty. I made three visits to the camp at the end of 1998, when there were fewer than a thousand inmates, but it had, they said, been much fuller. It was set off the coast road at a place called Calamocarro. You passed a row of fishing boats drawn up on the sandy beaches to your right and, a little way on, you could see a public phone box with a queue of Africans. You walked up over a steep gravel terrace to find dozens of Spanish Army tents pitched in a grove of eucalyptus.

By day, the camp had the generous, all-comer smell of the open markets in parts of Southern Africa: sweet soap; synthetic fabrics and weatherproof plastics trounced by rain; fritters; okra, oil and chili. The wind gusting off the sea rasped the eucalyptus, carrying the sharp, medicated scent beyond the confines of the settlement – a smell that I associated with the central provinces of Mozambique. There, in the 1980s, you encountered tens of thousands of refugees who didn't qualify as refugees, because they were fleeing, or resettled, inside the country's borders. Not many refugees in Calamocarro either: a person driven to the limit by poverty is not a refugee.

One section of the camp, however, consisted of a small Algerian detachment – a handful of tents containing perhaps twenty families, most of them fleeing the gun and the knife. In one tent a young couple and their three children had been installed for ten weeks, waiting for news of an asylum application. The mother was an educated 21-year-old from Oran who had been working before they left. Her father had been murdered by an Islamist faction the previous year; later she, too, had been threatened. Her husband was a security guard for the state petroleum company; as a government employee, he was also a target. They'd been relieved of their savings by the Moroccan frontier police and were now defenceless. It would not have done to send them back through Morocco to the butcher's war over the border.

The tension between the Algerians and sub-Saharans was unmistakable. Many sub-Saharans felt strongly that there should be some form of 'economic asylum' on the grounds that the atrophy of their economies had gone hand in hand with the erosion of human and political rights. They looked with a sidelong, suspect glance at the asylum seeker's bitter privilege. Others spoke well of the kindness they'd been shown while travelling through Algeria.

One morning in the camp, a giant of a man from Cameroon called Joseph announced that Algeria might be a dangerous place for Algerians, but 'not for us blacks'. He couldn't say why – 'Perhaps it's something in the Koran.' Joseph was 25. He had crossed most of the Sahara on foot and could tell you the time it had taken him, from the day he left home, to the day he reached Ceuta, with the precision of a man who had chalked up each sunrise on the floor of a vast, shimmering cell whose walls were an infinite distance from any point at which he woke. The total, which he was apt to repeat, came to 181 days. Joseph had nearly died of dehydration, but had been saved by nomads, who looked after him for a week or more and sent him on his way with a sack of powdered sugar and a skin of water. He insisted, in defence of the Algerians, that no one could know whether their asylum applications would be approved. He refused to join in a whispering campaign against them. Like several fellow Cameroonians, he was intent on mainland Europe. '*Je ferai n'importe quoi, pourvu que c'est légal.*' Though he had been driven north by poverty, he wanted to campaign for radical change in his country, just as any political exile might. Economic misery can make a dissident of almost anyone.

Joseph fraternised with the Algerians, towering over them like an illustrious tree, whose shade they invariably sought. He was on hand to argue their rights when it came to mealtimes – Spanish military rations delivered twice daily – or hustling for extra blankets, or barter disputes over home-made fritters and cigarettes. He also tended recent arrivals from West Africa. He took a man about ten years older than himself under his care as soon as he appeared in the camp: a courteous wraith in a green woollen hat emblazoned with a 'Red Raiders' logo. His complexion was floury after four months on the road and a long stint in the desert. 'You must be strong-backed to do this thing, especially going through Morocco,' he remarked while he waited for Joseph to negotiate a double helping of meat for him at the head of the food queue. 'They will take everything from you and beat you, I mean beat you so hard.' Moments later, his teeth began chattering and he gasped out a verdict on the journey he had made: 'No. Definitely I would not accept that my worst enemy should come this way.' He started laughing, then shaking, wrenching the hat from his head and coughing into it until I thought he would die, but when Joseph handed him a mountainous plate of food, he set about it with conviction.

There was something open-hearted and alert about these people who had crossed the desert. It seemed to give them the edge over the Algerians, who kept to their tents when they could, musing darkly over the bloodshed in which they'd been caught up, like so many of their fore-bears. Old stereotypes, almost obsolete now, were being revived by circumstance at this unlikely point of entry into Europe: the valiant African, the furtive Arab, the severe but tolerant white man, presiding over the destiny of the less provident races.

Calamocarro was an ill-lit place at night, full of milling, hooded shadows in anoraks. The ground was muddy, the air dank and the temperature too low for anyone's comfort. There were seldom more than two soldiers to oversee the throng of migrants. Apart from the odd scuffle, the camp was self-regulating, but in the darkness, it felt sombre and a little edgy. It was after dark, however, that people spoke freely and it would have been around seven or eight o'clock on a bitter night that Williams Osunde loomed out from the tent placements and introduced himself. Williams was 20. He had come from Lagos, where he threw over his studies when his father, then his extended family, were unable to support him. He drifted around for a time until it struck him that it was just no good: whichever way the cards fell, there was no future for him in Nigeria. One may as well come to an early end as waste away, so why not make the journey to Europe? 'Even we prefer dying here to dying there,' he said of the decision to leave. 'By now I was a realist, you see.'

Williams Osunde set out in a party of six, each of whom paid about £50 for a place on a 'camion' north to Sokoto. Here they paid another trucker to take them across the border and into Niger. Immigration at Niger relieved them of a further £50 per person. They hung about scraping funds together in Niger, working for peanuts as water-carriers and shoeshine boys, and meeting more young people from other parts of Nigeria, Ghana and Cameroon who were on the same trail. After two months in Niger they set off north on foot, 15 people by now. A six-day march brought them within striking distance of the Algerian border. They pooled their resources to engage the services of a trafficker, who took the money, put them in a truck but dropped them well short of the frontier. They walked the remaining 80 km.

At the frontier, they waited several days for an opportune moment to cross. Here, one of their party died of thirst. Williams no longer recalled the stages or the place names on the next leg of the journey. I think they would have continued on the road running north from Niger, pressed on through Algeria to In Salah and cut west to join another north-south road leading up to the Moroccan border – a journey of about 1800 km, some of it by truck, but most of it on foot. So far as they knew, and they were delirious for long periods, they crossed the Algerian Sahara in two months, the truck rides enabling them to strike an average of 30 km a day. By the time they entered Morocco, four more of their party had died.

Williams was about to describe what became of him in

Morocco, when an eerie voice some way behind him in the darkness began chanting: 'Row, row, row your boat, gently down the stream.' It broke off abruptly and a broad figure in a parka, face indistinguishable, was striding through the shadows towards us with one arm raised, as if in anger.

'Tell him, Williams,' said the voice in the depths of the parka, 'how our country produces 2.1 million barrels of oil a day and how we are starving. Nigeria, Federal Republic of Embezzlers.'

The young man in the parka had been one of Williams's party and now he urged him to divulge more detail about the journey. When Williams could not, or would not, it was his companion who explained how they had eaten leaves, sucked up the water from pools of sandy mud and drunk their own urine; how one of them was stabbed through the ribs during an argument with strangers and another had died of snakebite. He spoke of 'trekking' to the point of death, of seeming to die on his feet, falling into an abyss of exhaustion, only to be resurrected in the furnace of the late morning.

'Africans are strong,' said Williams. 'God just make them so.'

'Merrily, merrily, merrily, merrily . . .' the dark mouth in the shadow of the parka intoned, and again: 'Two point one million, my friend, two point one.'

At the Moroccan border, Williams and the remaining survivors were taken into custody by the police. Only one escaped.

'Upon all your suffering,' Williams concluded, 'upon all your trekking, upon all your danger, they will put you back.'

Like several people from other parties who had reached Calamocarro, they had been dumped by the Moroccans on the border with Algeria – 'l'Algérie, c'est par là' – and entered

Morocco later by another route, several days' hike further north. Everyone in the camp who was prepared to talk complained of ill-treatment in Morocco, and of being robbed of their last throw – a tradable watch, a low-carat gem, a nugget of gold – by the police. They claimed to have been beaten. And the three or four women – who had been brought along precisely because they were negotiating-counters in the event of an impasse – had been raped.

The last leg of the journey through Morocco to Ceuta brings those who have survived the Algerian desert and Moroccan hospitality to a low range of hills. Here they must wait, perhaps for several days, studying the Spanish military and police patrols around the border perimeter between the enclave and Morocco. Once there is a gap in the patrol schedule or propitious weather – low cloud, mist on the hills – they will make their bid for European territory. If they cross successfully and elude the chase, the great majority will be allowed to remain. Anyone caught on or near the perimeter is put back inside Morocco. Those are the rules. Success is a matter of luck and, eventually, persistence: nobody who has come this far will give up after one failure. In 1997, about 700 illegal migrants entered Ceuta this way. The tally for the following year was nearer 1000. For 1999, it was 7000. A year-on-year increase projected on these figures alone is intriguing. Most of the people who got across came overland; about 40 per cent – wealthier, one must assume – flew to Casablanca and made their way to the hills overlooking the perimeter with the help of Moroccan guides.

The EU knows that Ceuta and Melilla are vulnerable flanks of Fortress Europe, and that migrant pressure has to be opposed at these tempting points of transgression. In

1993 it approved funding for a defensive wall around Ceuta, running for eight kilometres and consisting of two parallel wire fences, 2.5 metres high and 5 metres apart. Between the wire fences a line of sensors was installed; lamps were set at every 33 metres and 30 closed circuit cameras spaced along the perimeter. Rolls of razor wire were laid beneath the nearside fence. Eighty-four culverts in the low ground where the border runs were cemented over. Round-the-clock patrols went into operation. The cost has been estimated at $25 million. Yet the long wire barrier stretching over the brown hills is no more than a term in the same game that sets clandestine migrants against wealthy countries further north: a kind of home line that has to be reached and surmounted, just as the trembling path of moonlight and the wake of the Italian patrol boats in the Otranto Channel are lines of jeopardy to be avoided. In both places the poor pit their wits against the technological expertise of the rich.

Alfonso Cruzado, the stocky, bespectacled officer of the Guardia Civil who showed me round the perimeter, suggested I scale one of the wire walls in the double defence. It took about 45 seconds. Balancing for the turn at the top, where the only handhold is a straight line of clipped wire, I punctured the palms of both hands. Cruzado said he had watched migrants take both fences in less than 20 seconds and wade through the razor wire, slashing their legs to shreds. If you have a bull at your back, he observed, then you're ready to run for your life. Like the British military involved in the withdrawal from Palestine, Cruzado and his colleagues were troubled by the fate to which they had abandoned their largest North African possession, the Spanish Sahara, in a botched decolonisation process that sent most of the inhabitants into indefinite exile. They saw the whole continent in the light of that failure and found it hard to put the burden of blame for its misfortunes on Africans.

'What colonial power seriously tried to develop an infrastructure in its African possessions?' Captain José Rebollo, one of Cruzado's superiors, asked when I suggested that the migrants who made it over the perimeter were very far from being downtrodden or defeated. He thought it wrong to attribute the force that drove them to their own strength of character when it was so evidently a material issue of misery – and history. Rebollo was hazy about the big picture but he was still on the right track.

'What power ever attempted to play down tribal differences?' he went on. 'And when Africa was distributed to the Europeans, was the division not done with a ruler? We, the colonial powers, are reaping what we sowed. The sub-Saharans who get here are people fleeing death and hunger.'

No one in the Guardia Civil appeared to disagree with this, and none believed the perimeter would be a match for such powerful motives or for such an intractable past. One or two said they liked to think that, faced with the problems sub-Saharans face, they would take the same course. They had a measured disdain for Moroccan illegals, whom they would turf back over the frontier, even if they were found inside the city – the Moroccans must face the perils of the Straits if they want to reach the EU, or try to hide in trucks on the ferries: hundreds of young stowaways are caught and returned every year. The Guardia Civil were not keen, either, on wealthier sub-Saharans, chiefly from francophone countries, who they claimed to have found with mobile phones and assets of several thousand dollars in Calamocarro. On the rest, however, they looked sympathetically, even conscientiously.

So did the civilian administration in Ceuta. The Spanish authorities undertake to 'regularise' migrants who reach the enclave and, if possible, to find them jobs. There are weekly work details and, in due course, as the paperwork on each migrant is completed, a one-year renewable work permit allows them onto the Spanish mainland – a mixture of realism and civility that is absent in other EU member states and also at odds with EU policy.

As for the perimeter, neither civilian nor military personnel thought of it as a barrier. The expensive high-tech edifice at the margins of Fortress Europe was a filter only, which might thin down the numbers of uninvited to about 300 a year. This was a target figure from the Governor's office, yet the spokesman who supplied it was doubtful. 'Directly beneath us,' he said, 'is a continent in crisis. It's not yet alarming, but it's going to grow, slowly, incrementally, and we must prepare for something very much larger.' He was working on the assumption that by 2014 anything between 15 and 20 million migrants would have made a bid for entry into Western Europe via Spain.

Rebollo, an old military man with a soldier's interest in history, saw things in much the same way. Migration had usually been from poor parts of the world to richer ones – 'What was it that drove the Barbarians to Rome?' he asked – but he was persuaded that migrations from the North lacked the staying power of those from the South. It was a very Spanish perspective, which he brought up to date by citing the per capita GDP of Morocco ($1200) relative to that of Spain ($15,000) – a modest difference, as it happens, beside the comparative purchasing power of an Austrian citizen (75.7 in PPP), against that of a Nigerian (3.0) or a Sierra Leonean (1.4). Rebollo felt that something had to give. To predict how it would happen, he had used the push-pull model of migration to imagine a one-way hurricane whose early warning was a spate of dust-devils wriggling north across the scrublands of the Sahel.

In 1999, the perimeter around Ceuta was deemed inadequate against the low technologies of willpower and mutiny. The authorities decided to increase the surveillance capacity along its length – more cameras, better sensors – in the hope that the numbers who get across will dwindle to a level that the EU finds acceptable. Increasingly, sub-Saharan migrants, like many Moroccans, have been forced to contemplate the frightening option of the Straits, or to work their way up the 'right side' of the continent, forging a more dependable chain of contacts as they head into the arms of the Levantine traffickers.

Europe, meanwhile, has devised a very fine form of 'sieving' for illegal migrants from Africa: by reaching the safety of the camp, the able and resourceful define the quality of the intake. They, in turn, are drawn from a larger contingent who self-selected earlier on by leaving their countries of origin and submitting to the trans-Saharan ordeal. Many survivors of the Sahara, moreover, have already selfselected from the hundreds of thousands who abandon the harsh conditions of rural Africa for those of Lagos, Accra, Abidjan, Kinshasa, Bamako, Yaoundé, Dakar. Whether they end up picking fruit in Almería, cleaning the toilets in the Bibliothèque Nationale, running a UN Agency in Geneva, a prostitution ring in Milan or an African Studies course in the Netherlands, these job-seekers are among the most highly motivated in Europe.

*

There is something puzzling about sub-Saharan Africa's place in the pattern of intercontinental migration. The anecdotal evidence of those Africans who have made it to Europe reinforces the crude model of desperation as the great push – as strong as any more sophisticated ambition, fired by the rise of a regional economy, or the decline of a superpower. Yet, if it is true that things in Africa can get no worse – as the optimists concluded in the mid-1990s – then in due course the numbers of migrants will increase. Rebollo and his men will have been right for the wrong reasons. War, hunger, social breakdown and economic collapse have not produced demographic eruptions beyond the natural boundary of the Sahara, but the first shafts of prosperity may.

What, though, if Rebollo were right for the reasons he gave? After all, 'globalisation' has yet to hold a candle up to history. It is a latecomer on the scene and many of its consequences are still unclear. It is quite possible that one of its effects, in due course, will be to blur, or complicate, the recent picture of international migration, in which abject poverty does not produce the same degree of migratory pressure from developing countries as relative wealth. The ambiguities, at that point, might merely multiply, so that migrants from the poorest economies begin to press towards rich states with more insistence, alongside others who have already taken their cue from an increase in living standards.

As the contradiction becomes more apparent, what might wealthier states conclude, if not that the more prosperous an economic area and the more stable the politics that attend that prosperity, the less inclined people will be to seek out an entirely new life, once and for all, in an enclave of wealth thousands of miles from their homes? Yet this is the most simple-minded vision of poor-to-rich migration – the layman's elementary model, which geographers and demographers have spent decades revising. Is it stupidity that leads the layman back to it, or obstinacy, or – in the present 'global' configuration – merely the sense that it would be rash to rule out poverty as one of the factors that forces human beings across continents? When we come back to the notion that severe hardship still plays a part in migration, we also come back to our senses.

Perhaps, too, we come back to an older truth about human movement, stirring beneath the huge weight of scholarly work on migration – a truth we begin to grasp when, at the end of an unimaginable journey, a young woman from West Africa in the seventh month of her pregnancy scales two high fences, fights her way through a roll of razor wire and enters Europe by a little Spanish garrison in the Maghreb. This petitioner at the rich man's gate was one of a dozen or more who crossed into Ceuta while I was going in and out of the camp at Calamocarro. She was caught on the perimeter road and it looked very much as if she knew the rules of the game: the Guardia Civil had planned to make an exception in her case – or so they said – but when they put her in a cell overnight before transferring her to the camp, she committed suicide. Nobody established her country of origin or even her real name.

For a day or two her death was all over the Spanish press. It also stirred up a passionate sense of solidarity in Calamocarro. Williams Osunde was so distressed by the news that he insisted on attending the funeral, though he had never met her. At the graveside he read from Ephesians: 'For we wrestle not against the flesh and blood, but against principalities, against powers, against the rulers of the darkness of this world, against spiritual wickedness in high places.' The way Williams saw it, there were two domains, that of the rich and that of the poor; and there was a scandalous conspiracy to ensure that those from the second who needed to reach the first were prevented from doing so.

Injustice is the moral force in this account. But it also restores necessity to its central role in the story of human movement, referring back to older, more local migrations in Africa and other parts of the world, where mobility was bound up with the search for pasture. When you stand at the fringes of Fortress Europe and gaze into Morocco, in the knowledge that at any moment there are at least four or five people concealed in the folds of the hills or lying low in tiny huts, watching the Spanish border patrols and weighing up their moment, the idea of necessity is impossible to set aside. Day after day, year after year, the members of the Guardia Civil in Ceuta and Melilla scrutinise the terrain on the other side of their frontiers. No argument is likely to shake their belief in the idea that it is lack and fear that drive people north to trespass on the lush grasslands of mainland Europe.

In the epic story of Sundiata, the 13th-century warrior-king who founds the ancient empire of Mali, the hero begins life as a cripple. The blacksmiths forge crutches for him, but they buckle when he tries to use them. On the day before his circumcision, however, Sundiata raises his arms, grips the eaves of his mother's house and pulls himself upright. He reaches out to a baobab tree, tears it from the ground and sets it down at the doorway of the house. In this dramatic transition from broken child to emperor, the extent of an earlier debility measures precisely the extent of a new strength. Like Sundiata, the champions who manage to reach Europe by luck and endurance have wrung strength from weakness, but they have had to draw on the kinds of fundamental resources that are not replenished automatically. And, whatever else they are, they remain fugitives, just as anyone trying to escape the clutches of a dictatorship, or a party of religious zealots, is a fugitive. In the past, refugees have won greater international sympathy than economic migrants. Theirs has been the more identifiable grievance: at its source there is often an identifiable persecutor. Yet the order of economic difficulty that prevails in some parts of the world is akin to persecution. No consensus exists about the identity of the tormentor, and so those who try to put it behind them are more easily reviled than others fleeing the attentions of secret police or state militias.

Little solace here for the economic migrant, even though the resolve of poorer people to breach the walls of the wealthy economies has a political character, for it involves defiance as well as despair. It is not their political opinion, so much as their political predicament that puts them in danger. Their first enemy is grinding attrition in their own country; their second, more formidable adversary is to be found in the countries on which they have set their hearts, where governments still move with a pitiful sloth towards debt cancellation and fair trade, and where the illegal migrant is regarded as a cutpurse. Most people who migrate away from misery are politicised; they have the facts and figures somewhere at the back of their minds. A man like Joseph who set out from Cameroon in 1998 to look for a job in Europe would have known that his country's debt stood at nine billion dollars, and that every year the sum of interest and principal due for repayment was higher than national export earnings. He would have despised his government as a coterie of irresponsible villains. He would have seen many lives turn to dust. He would also have understood that none of this could amount to mitigation, in the eyes of the rich world, once he forced his way in. Realising in the end that he was on his own, he would have struck out anyhow, to take whatever he could get.

NOTES AND ACKNOWLEDGMENTS

I have tried not to encumber this book with figures, but there are a good many. Some of the sources are given below.

For international human movement, *World Migration Report 2000*, Geneva, International Organisation for Migration (IOM), 2000.

For people arriving illegally on the coast of Italy, 1998-99, the Guardia di Finanza offices in Otranto and *The Economist*, 16 October 1999.

For revenue in illegal trafficking worldwide, Jonas Widgren, 'The Multilateral Co-Operation to Combat Trafficking in Migrants, 11th IOM Seminar on Migration', IOM, 1994.

For UN refugee resettlement between the 1970s and 1990s, and stateless persons in the 1990s, *The State of the World's Refugees: A Humanitarian Agenda* (UNHCR/Oxford, 1997).

For sex-workers trafficked into the EU, Phil Williams (ed), *Illegal Immigration and Commercial Sex: The New Slave Trade* (Frank Cass, 1999); for details on Amsterdam, the essay by Bruinsma and Meershoek, 'Organised Crime and Trafficking in Women from East Europe in the Netherlands'.

For movements in Europe from the late 19th century until the early 1950s, John Hope Simpson (ed), *The Refugee Problem: Report of a Survey* (Oxford, 1939); Tony Kushner and Katharine Knox, *Refugees in an Age of Genocide* (Frank Cass, 1999) and Hannah Arendt, *The Origins of Totalitarianism* (Harcourt Brace Jovanovich, 1973), especially Chapter 9, 'The Decline of the Nation-State and the Origins of Totalitarianism'.

For percentages of Zaireans, Sri Lankans and Somalis receiving refugee status in Canada and the UK during the 1990s, and research staff available to adjudicators in the UK and Australia, *Providing Protection: Towards Fair and Effective Asylum Procedures* (Justice/Immigration Law Practitioners' Association/Asylum Rights Campaign, 1997).

For Bosnian asylum seekers in and out of Germany, total asylum applications in Germany in 1992 and deaths of clandestine migrants in Europe now (and in the future),the invaluable *Migration News Sheet*, 205 rue Belliard, B-1040 Brussels (by subscription, fax: +32 2 230 37 50).

For the numbers of blacks and Asians entering the UK from the late 1950s onwards, Ian Spencer, *British Immigration Policy Since 1939* (Routledge, 1997).

For percentages of settlement applications refused by the UK, Joint Council for the Welfare of Immigrants et al., Conference statement 'British Immigration Policy: A Legacy of Racism?', (26 October 1999).

For Home Office figures for UK asylum applications and appeals in 1997, 'UK Asylum Laws: Before and After' (*BBC News Online*, 24 August 1999).

For unsuccessful asylum applicants staying on in Britain, Immigration Service Union (20 August 1997), cited in the *Bulletin of the Joint Council for the Welfare of Immigrants* (Summer 1998).

Numbers of Afghan asylum applications and refusals in Europe were supplied by the Refugee Council.

For digests of the Human Development Index and the PPP tables, as well as country statistics for Belgium, Guinea and Cameroon, *Pocket World in Figures 2000* (Profile/*The Economist*, 1999).

For immigrants living in Europe, sub-Saharans living outside the continent and the global value of remittances, Libercier and Schneider, *Migrants: Partners in Development Co-Operation* (Panos Institute/OECD, Paris, 1996).

For forthcoming shortages of under-65s in rich countries, *Trends in International Migration*, annual report for 1998, Paris, OECD.

For guest-worker totals in Germany, Stephen Castles and Mark Miller, *The Age of Migration* (Macmillan, 1993).

For Chinese migrant labour to the Americas, Gérard Chaliand and Jean-Pierre Rageau, *The Penguin Atlas of Diasporas* (Viking Penguin, 1995).

For entries, legal and attempted illegal, into Ceuta and mainland Spain and detainees in Calamocarro, the Governor's Office, Ceuta in November 1998 and February 2000.

Non-statistical material is based on a number of sources.

For the growth of trafficking, John Morrison, *The Cost of Survival* (London, The Refugee Council, 1998).

The 1951 Convention and the 1967 Protocol relating to the Status of Refugees are published in the *Handbook of Procedures and Criteria for Determining Refugee Status* (Geneva, UNHCR, 1979 with subsequent editions).

For stories of Somali traffickers, Nuruddin Farah, *Yesterday, Tomorrow: Voices from the Somali Diaspora* (Cassell, 2000).

For official defamation of Albanians in the Tito and post-Tito periods, Julie Mertus, *Kosovo: How Myths and Truths Started a War* (Berkeley, 1999).

For the 1951 Convention and the Cold War, the essay by Danièle Joly in Part Four of *Refugee Rights and Realities: Evolving International Concepts and Regimes*, edited by Frances Nicholson and Patrick Twomey (Cambridge, 1999).

For the story of the *Cheshire*, the evacuation of Belgians to Britain in 1914, the anti-Belgian riots and the revolt of the Basque children in Kent, Kushner and Knox, 1999.

For the British press on asylum seekers, the *Daily Mail*, 3 February 1900 (quoted in Kushner and Knox) and 6 October 1998; the *Dover Express*, 1 October 1998 and the *Jewish Chronicle*, 4 June 1999.

For the rise of the 'colour bar' in the UK, Ian Spencer, 1997.

For the story of the Ugandan trader turned asylum seeker, Hirit Belai, *London Review of Books* (18 July 1996).

For the 'Kosovar' African in Calais, *Libération*, 22 August 1999.

For recommendations on improved asylum procedures in the UK, *Providing Protection* (Justice/ILPA/ARC).

W.H. Auden's poem appears untitled as the first of the 'Ten Songs' in *Collected Poems* (Faber, 1991).

For the Amsterdam Treaty, Ben Hall and Ashish Bhatt, *Policing Europe: EU Justice and Home Affairs Co-Operation* (London, Centre for European Reform, 1999).

The 'draft action plans' of the High Level Working Group were discussed at a special meeting of the European Council in Tampere on 15 and 16 October 1999.

PART II

For background on indigenous Italian migration, John Foot, 'Immigration and the City: Milan and mass immigration, 1958-98' in *Modern Italy*, 4 (2), 1999.

John Berger and Jean Mohr, *A Seventh Man*, was published by Penguin.

Susan George, *The Lugano Report: On Preserving Capitalism in the 21st Century* was published by Pluto, 1999.

For Yaguine Koita and Fodé Tounkara, Alex Duval Smith in *The Independent*, 1 September 1999.

For Germany's struggle with 'citizenship', Christian Joppke, *Immigration and the Nation State*, (Oxford, 1999).

E.G. Ravenstein's analysis of the 1871 census of the British Isles was reprinted from the *Geographical Magazine* as *The Birthplaces of the People and the Laws of Migration* by Trübner, 1876.

For migrants and 'co-development', Libercier and Schneider, 1996.

The arguments about economic growth in 'sender countries' tending to generate migrants can be found in two key works on modern migration: Saskia Sassen, *The Mobility of Labor and Capital* (Cambridge, 1988), especially Chapter 4, and Nigel Harris, *The New Untouchables: Immigration and the New World Worker* (I.B. Tauris, 1995), especially Chapter 7.

Several people read over the manuscript of this book and suggested a number of important changes: Laurie Fransman, Lorna Scott Fox, David Styan, Peter Marsden, Imran Hussain and Sue Candler of the Refugee Council. Don Flynn of the Joint Council for the Welfare of Immigrants, who also read the manucript, was a generous provider of knowledge and good sense. I am also grateful to Andrew Franklin and Profile, and to Peter Campbell. I'm indebted, above all, to Mary-Kay Wilmers and my colleagues at the *London Review of Books* for turning a pile of paper into a presentable set of thoughts.

Part of The Uninvited was first published in the London Review of Books on 3 February 2000. The London Review of Books may be ordered through your local newsagent or taken on subscription. For subscriptions please call 020 7209 1141 or fax 020 7209 1151.